Pretty much everything
you need to know about...

Working with 5–7s

Colin Draper
Helen Franklin
Sara O'Shea

Scripture Union, 207–209 Queensway, Bletchley, MK2 2EB, England.
Email: info@scriptureunion.org.uk
Website: www.scriptureunion.org.uk

Scripture Union Australia
Locked Bag 2, Central Coast Business Centre, NSW 2252
Website: www.su.org.au

Scripture Union USA
PO Box 987, Valley Forge, PA 19482
Website: www.scriptureunion.org

Unless otherwise stated, Bible quotations are taken from the Contemporary English Version ©American Bible Society 1991, 1992, 1995. Anglicisations ©British and Foreign Bible Society 1996. Published in the UK by HarperCollins*Publishers* and used with permission.

British Library Cataloguing-in-Publication Data.
A catalogue record for this book is available from the British Library.

Printed and bound in Great Britain by Nuffield Press.
Cover: Phil Grundy
Internal design: 3T Creative
Photographs: Silhouettes of kids in motion, Rubberball productions copyright © 2002

Children's prayers are taken from *Hey God...wot u up 2?*, Salvation Army 2006.
Used with permission.

Contents

Introduction

The children in the 5 to 7s group were invited to suggest a song to be included in the church's service the following week. There was silence for a moment, and then six-year-old Billy piped up.
'Can we sing "YMCA"?' he asked.

Whether you read this book from cover to cover or just dip into it, join us in celebrating the delights of working with children of this age, many of whom still have about them a sense of naivety and openness. Yet they are also capable of remarkably mature thinking. We will tackle many of the issues involved in such work and seek to find some solutions.

The Jesuit motto says, 'Give me the child until he is seven and I will give you the man.' What a privilege to be involved with God in shaping lives to this extent!

Dedication:
To Beryl, Laura and Nathan who keep me grounded in the real world. (Colin)

To Lizzie, with huge love and thanks for all that you teach me about children. (Helen)

To Kelvin and my two amazing children, Lawrence and Niamh, who are the reason why I teach. (Sara)

How to use this book

We all learn differently, so feel free to use this book in a number of ways. You might want to read through the whole book from beginning to end, or dip in and out, referring to the chapters that meet your immediate need (although I hope you'll go back and read the others too!). I would encourage you to go through this book with other 5 to 7s leaders in your team. Why not use it as the basis of a series of training sessions for those working with 5 to 7s in your church?

You will notice that the left-hand pages contain slightly more in-depth text, while the right-hand pages concentrate more on practical information and activities. These are designed to help you work through some of the issues raised on the left-hand page. Right-hand pages contain:

> Bible boxes: key passages to look up, and ideas to help you engage with them, either individually or as a group of 5 to 7s leaders.

> Action boxes: something practical for you to think about or do alongside reading this book. So, for example, if you've been reading about the world of 5 to 7s on the left-hand page, the action box on the right-hand page might suggest watching a range of TV programmes for the age group.

> Contact boxes: these contain cross references to relevant organisations, websites etc.

Chapter Link

Chapter links: to point you to other places in the book that deal with related issues.

Colin Draper and Helen Franklin have many years' experience in evangelism and schools' work for Scripture Union and have led SU's 5 to 7s programme at Spring Harvest. Sara O'Shea is an experienced teacher of Key Stage 1 children and has led the 5 to 7s work at her church holiday club.

Chapter 1 – Perspectives on 5 to 7s

Six-year-old Joanna was asked what would help her to know Jesus better. She thought about it for a short while and then a smile stretched across her face. Joanna was quite certain of her answer. 'Have Jesus come for a sleepover!' she replied enthusiastically.

Joanna's answer tells us a lot about her. She is:
- Sociable.
- Good at thinking.
- Keen on talking (likes the chattiness of a sleepover).
- What we often call 'bright' – she works out the answer quite quickly.
- Imaginative.
- A child of her time – sleepovers are quite the thing, even for 6-year-olds these days!

Is that the sort of picture that comes to mind when you think about 5- to 7-year-olds? What general characteristics stand out? Perhaps you have vivid memories of your own early years that help to form this picture. Pause before you read any more and fill in the characteristics that stand out for you on the opposite page, and the 'I remember …' reflections on page 9.

Our perspective

Of course what we remember of our childhood will be very different from what today's children will remember when they are adults! Things change so fast that the contents of a child's toy box today will soon make an appearance in the local charity shop, no longer wanted. Technology develops at such a rate that we cannot even imagine what it will allow us to do in five years' time, never mind 20 years from now. We simply cannot put our own childhood alongside that of today's generation of 5-, 6- and 7-year-olds and make comparisons. Or can we?

Despite the major changes that take place in society, technology and education between different generations, some things remain the same about these middle years of childhood:
- The importance of love and family life;
- The value of learning and discovery;
- The scope of imagination when it is fuelled and allowed to flow;
- The truth that each child is loved by God.

As people who want to help children of this age to discover the love of Jesus and live in the fullness of it, we need to grasp both the changing and the unchanging. We need to help children face the challenges of change through the strength that comes from the unchanging. In this book we will look at the world in which children live, the influences that impact them and consider the ways in which we need to relate to and work with them in order to help them 'grasp how wide and long and high and deep is the love of Christ, and to know this love that surpasses knowledge'. (Ephesians 3:18,19 NIV)

The characteristics of 5- to 7-year olds

On your own (or with others in your 5-7 team) write down in this outline as many of the characteristics of each age that you can think of or choose just one key characteristic for each age.

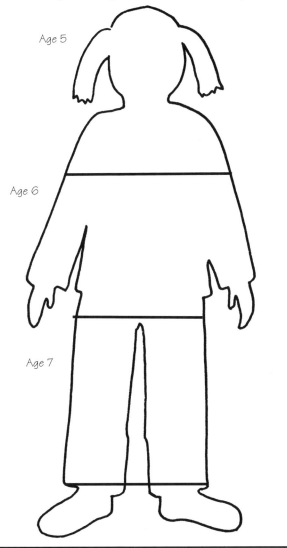

Age 5

Age 6

Age 7

The very fact that you are reading this book probably means that you already have a positive image of 5- to 7-year-olds. But not everyone shares our views. In this first chapter we shall look at the ways that different groups of people see and treat children of this age and what affect that has on the children.

5 to 7s and society

As a rule, 21st century British society does not make much of 5- to 7-year-olds. Children in general feature quite highly, but this age group are often somewhat ignored. Their younger siblings are well catered for with specialist shops, groups, and a multitude of toys to help them learn. Their older siblings who have reached the dizzy heights of 8 and above have much more available to them by way of reading matter, computer games, sports and toys. Many of these items require complex manipulation by dextrous hands. Also, being more independent, the world is bigger and wider because they can do so much more.

Television channels are given over to the needs of under 5s but most programmes for 5 to11s suit the needs of those at the older end of the spectrum. That may be in part because children are more likely to watch something that is geared for an older age group than a younger one.

At this age they are too big for toddlers' play equipment in the park, even though it may still have an appeal. It is familiar and therefore probably much loved. They are also too small for the more exciting rides at the funfair that the braver ones would dearly love to try out. Age and height restrictions mean that they can only watch and not participate in some activities provided for children. Being 5, 6 or 7 can be a time of frustration while they wait for younger or older siblings who are busily engaged in activities that are not allowed for 5 to 7s.

Society generally rates its members by their achievements and contributions, and in this sense some would say that 5 to 7s have little to offer. Younger children are 'cute' and not expected to be able to do things; older children can do things, however, and so have their place by right. But 5 to 7s? It can seem as if their role is simply to grow up!

5 to 7s and teachers

When Tom began his second year of teaching a class of Year 1 children, who would all reach their sixth birthday during the academic year, he was astonished to discover how little they knew. His comment was, 'I didn't realise how much I had taught my last class in the year!'

The years in school from Reception to Year 2 are some of the most learning-packed years of a child's educational experience. Some children will arrive in school barely able to recognise their own name or to draw anything that is recognisable. Hopefully they will move on to Key stage 2 (Years 3 to 6) with the ability to read and write and to understand the basics of how to add, subtract, multiply and divide and to apply that in everyday life. They will know how to operate a computer (although many will have learnt that skill in relation to games before even arriving in school), and have a reasonable knowledge and understanding of the world around them from Science, History and Geography lessons. They will have greater physical

When I was at infant school, I remember…

Record your memories of being 5 to 7.

coordination and be able to play simple games with a partner using equipment, having developed socially by playing and learning with others both in class and in the playground. They will also be able to talk more confidently with their peers and adults who are familiar to them in a range of different settings. This is due in no small part to the dedication, hard work and care of their teachers.

Helen says: I have yet to meet an Infants' teacher who does not spend a great deal of time outside the classroom preparing materials to teach this age group and thinking of ways to enrich their education. One teacher I know thinks carefully about what she wears as well as what she does; she has a whole range of badges and brooches – teddy bears, flowers, animals – so that she can wear a different one every day, because the children notice them and like this.

As we work with this age group we can learn much from those who teach them in school, both in terms of the way that schools work with them, the depth of learning they achieve and the way that they make discoveries. But we can also learn from their approach to the children – the tone of voice and level of language that they use, their methods for keeping control and drawing out quiet children, their understanding of the children's lives.

5 to 7s and parents

Our hope and prayer is that every parent will think the world of their 5-, 6- or 7-year-old, as indeed of any son or daughter they may have. Reality tells us that this is not always the case, but we are going to consider a child typical of this age group who is loved by their parents. In part, a parent's view will be slightly different between their firstborn and successive children. With the first child everything is new and the parent is learning as much as the child. But with every successive child there is a degree of familiarity, however different the children may be.

Unsurprisingly, there are both positive and negative results from being either the eldest or only child.

Positively:
- Parents have more time to spend with a first child, although they may have a myriad of other responsibilities as well.
- They have no rival for parental attention.
- They are more likely to be praised for their achievements, as these are eagerly awaited by keen family members.
- They will be more likely to have new clothes and toys.

There are some implications for us here. It would be a generalisation to say that all firstborn or only children are spoilt, but we may see signs of difficult behaviour if a child always gets their own way at home, or is treated more like a miniature adult because they are the only child in the home.

Chapter Link

Chapter 2 has a section on school from a child's viewpoint. Chapter 3 covers what and how children learn in school.

Negatively:
- They are the trailblazers, with whom parents are more likely to be cautious than with successive children.
- They are on the receiving end of novice parenting skills. In Britain, we demand that people take both theory and practical tests before driving a car, yet there is no set level of attainment for being a parent!
- If they are the first, but not the only child, their needs may have to be put on hold for younger siblings who need feeding, changing and holding more often. For example, 5-year-olds are too old for the picture books that they enjoyed in nursery but still need help to read words, yet this may not always be possible when their parents are busy with other tasks.

As people who work with children we may need to give a child of this age more attention when a younger sister or brother is born, if they feel neglected at home. We may notice a big difference between children in the group depending on where they come in age order amongst their family.

These are just some of the issues impacting firstborn children at this age. Of course there are plenty that affect subsequent children too, such as the fact that they:
- May receive less parental attention;
- May be slower in developing skills, eg reading;
- May be quicker because they learn much from older siblings;
- Are often more sociable because they are used to playing with older siblings;
- Often have toys and clothes that are passed down to them;
- Are often less responsible.

5 to 7s and the wider family
It may also be the case that firstborn children receive more attention from their wider family than do successive siblings or cousins. New grandparents in particular will dote especially on their first grandchild, and with so many children being cared for by grandparents at some point in the average week, we may well find ourselves dealing with them. As we work with children we will do well to see them through the eyes of the wider family who may celebrate their triumphs and tolerate their tantrums far more than we do! We may find, too, that grandparents have stricter views about childcare than parents, 'we didn't do it like that!', and they may not always like the way things are done today. We need to avoid being caught up in intergenerational arguments within families!

5 to 7s and siblings
As indicated in the previous sections, much depends on whether a child has older or younger siblings – or both. Middle children are often much more placid than either the eldest or youngest, perhaps because they are so used to being in the middle that they take the middle ground in most things!

Prayer for 5-7s

Thank God

If you work regularly with 5- to 7-year-olds, thank God for each one, pausing to picture them. Think of one thing that makes each child stand out in your mind. If you do not have a particular group of children in mind, thank God for what children of this age bring to society.

Pray for those who influence 5 to 7s

Pray for those who have the greatest influence on 5 to 7s: their family and teachers, their carers and other professionals, the media, their friends and their families. Pray that they would have wisdom in bringing up and educating these children. Ask God to give each one love, patience and the ability to listen to children.

Pray for the 5 to 7s you know

Think of the 5-to 7-year-olds that you know best. Pray for their development, health and happiness. and for them to know God and to grow in that knowledge and in their friendship with Jesus.

Ask their parents' permission to take a photograph of them; create a montage of these photos to remind you to pray regularly.

In reality we cannot make generalisations. We can neither assume that all children from one family will be the same, nor that all eldest or youngest children in different families will behave in similar ways. Eldest children are often given responsibility for their younger siblings, but the impact of this is hard to predict. Some will take this responsibility seriously and it will flow over into other activities, while others, freed from the need to be responsible, will be more mischievous. Some youngest children will grow up quickly, eager to keep up with their older brothers and sisters, whilst others will be so used to having everything done for them that they are slower at taking responsibility for themselves.

Another important factor that can affect behaviour is the age gap between children. On the opposite page, read about the age gap experience in two families.

Lessons for us from all of this include:
• Never assume that one child in a family will behave or achieve just the same as another.
• Know families as well as possible to be aware of any situation that could cause unusual behaviour.
• Never call a child by their sibling's name!

5 to 7s on 5 to 7s

How do children in this age group see each other?

As we will consider in chapter 3, these are years of huge change and growth. You could argue that all childhood years are, but these years present a special challenge: they are becoming aware of the differences in each other. At this age James will notice when his friends Jessica and Jordan are reading books with more words on each page than his book has. Jessica will recognise that at the swimming baths Jordan can now swim unaided whilst she and James can only splash around, doggy-paddle style, if their armbands are removed. When it comes to football James is in an under 7s team, but Jordan still forgets that the ball is meant to be kicked, and instead picks it up to throw it – or more often keeps it for himself. Even when he does kick it he has no sense of playing together with the other boys as a team: whenever the ball is loose they all converge on it, rather than one child racing for it and passing it to others. The children are well aware of these differences, and the closer they get to the age of 7, the more the differences concern them. They do not like to stand out for what they cannot do, although they enjoy being different because they have developed new skills.

In practice, this means that we will need to offer a range of activities to suit children's different abilities, and a variable amount of help to enable them to complete them. Those who can work unaided will be indignant if offered help, whilst those whose hands have still not mastered scissors may want us to cut out their craft so that they can at least achieve something that looks as good as their friend's model.

It also requires us to encourage them by praising their achievements, always judging these

Case study on age gaps in a family

Tim is 7. He has been given a magician's kit for his birthday and is slowly mastering the tricks. He is eager to put on a magic show for any visitors who come and has made up a clever rhyming patter for these shows. 'Cheese and biscuits, pop and beer, make this marble disappear!' cries Tim as he performs his trick. Everyone is impressed and they clap enthusiastically. Lucy, Tim's 3-year-old sister, does not want to miss out on all this attention. So when he has finished showing his tricks she puts on a dance show, which receives equally rapturous applause.

Daniel, who is almost 8, received a similar magician's box for Christmas and has practised the tricks until he can perform them convincingly. His sister Lauren is 2 years younger and loves to copy him. But she is not as adept at the tricks and annoys him intensely when she tries to perform one and gives away the secret of how it is done to their audience. Their proud family are equally impressed by both, as each child performed at the level appropriate for their age. But Daniel is cross that Lauren has spoilt the show, and she, who adores her big brother, is hurt that he has reacted in this way.

Why such a difference in outcome when the two stories are almost the same? Lauren is eager to keep up with Daniel and so invades his territory, whereas Lucy simply does what she enjoys and happily lets Tim perform his tricks. Tim views her as still being 'little' and therefore is quite protective of her, whereas Daniel sees Lauren as a threat because they are closer in age. He wants to prove that he is older and better, whilst she is trying to match him.

Of course when Tim was five and Lucy just one, she was the cause of many tears as she took her first steps and knocked down his carefully constructed Lego models. Tim was very proud of his achievements and unaware that his parents were equally delighted with Lucy's new-found ability to walk. But as Tim has grown older he has become more tolerant, and Lucy is learning to be careful – although he might still cry if she ruined something he had spent hours constructing!

by what the same child had previously been able to do, not by comparison with another child of the same age.

5 to 7s and the Church

Christine was troubled by a difficult working relationship with a colleague. There was constant friction and Christine, in charge of her section, was struggling to help the staff work together efficiently and harmoniously. One Sunday at church she asked the prayer team to pray with her about the situation. This particular church encouraged children to go round with the adults on the prayer team to watch, learn and pray too. As the team prayed, tears ran down Christine's cheeks, but a small hand took hold of hers and kept hold of it throughout the prayers. When the prayer team moved on, the perceptive 5-year-old who had offered this comfort stayed with Christine until she stopped crying.

There are not too many churches where children as young as 5 are allowed the opportunity to be part of prayer ministry either passively or actively. Should they do so? Some would argue that young children should not be used in prayer ministry because of the potential that they may hear things that are unsuitable for them at this age.

Yet younger children often know by instinct when someone is upset and in need of comfort, and at this age they know nothing of the fear of either being rejected or laughed at that would cause an older child or adult to hesitate before offering help. They see and respond intuitively, often in just the right way. At the age of 5 Adam was often aware when his friends were upset or hurt and would put a concerned hand on their arm as he asked, 'Lovey, are you all right?' in just the same gentle tones and words as his mother used to him. Children could bring so much to pastoral care if they were only given a chance, but few churches will take that 'risk', believing them to be too young to be used by God.

Instead, many people in churches will consider children of this age group as only able to colour pictures or listen to Bible stories; they would not even consider allowing children to have an important role in the church's worship. And even when they do, all too often they applaud the children for their part. This is fine for boosting the children's self-esteem and confidence, but the message it gives is that they have just 'entertained the congregation', not led them. Would they clap the pastor after an inspirational sermon or cheer after a good prayer? Not if it was led by an adult! So for many children, church is a place of limitation, frustration, boredom and dissatisfaction. But at this point, pause and consider the questions on the opposite page to help you think about your church's reaction to younger children.

5 to 7s and the Bible

What does God think of children aged 5, 6 or 7? Since the Bible makes no specific mention of children of this age we can only draw conclusions from texts that speak of God in relation to all children. But the picture that we build up is a very good one: of knowledge, care, love and concern for a child's growth in every aspect of their life and faith. Reflect on the verses on page 19.

Checklist: 5-7s and your church

Approximately what percentage of your church are aged 5 to 7?

How does your church show children of this age that they are welcome there?

What opportunities are there for contact between 5 to 7s and adult members of the congregation other than their parents?

How often and for how long do children of this age participate in worship with the rest of the congregation?

What helps them to feel and be involved?

What hinders their engagement with what is happening?

Are the parts of the service when they are present suitable for them?

Does your church involve children aged 5 to 7 in leading worship? How is their contribution received?

Chapter Link

In chapter 8 we will look in more detail at the issues of children and church.

Children aged 5 to 7 must have been present on many crucial occasions in the lives of God's people:

- Among those who fled from Pharaoh's rule in Egypt after the angel of death passed over their homes.
- Among those who crossed the Jordan into the Promised Land a generation later.
- Another generation were doubtless among the crowds when the ark was brought to the temple.
- A later generation were exiled into Babylon.
- Their descendants would have been among the children who rejoiced when the re-built walls of Jerusalem were dedicated under Nehemiah. Some may have been amongst those 'who were able to understand' when the Book of the Law had been read to the people.

In New Testament times we assume that there would be some children present when Jesus fed 5,000 men. Also, Matthew implies that children were among the crowds who put palm branches in the road to welcome Jesus. He records that, later in the day at the temple:

'The chief priests and the teachers of the Law of Moses were angry when they saw his miracles and heard the children shouting praises to the Son of David. The men said to Jesus, "Don't you hear what those children are saying?" "Yes, I do!" Jesus answered. "Don't you know that the Scriptures say, 'Children and infants will sing praises'?"' (Matthew 21:15,16)

You can just see 5 to 7s, full of enthusiasm and jumping up and down with excitement – though perhaps unaware of what was happening! But does that matter? Not at all. Most of us have memories of experiences from those years of childhood that are etched in our minds because of what happened, but only understood with hindsight and the wisdom that comes from hearing others talk about the events later.

A Biblical basis for work with 5 to 7s

In the Old Testament

Deuteronomy 6 outlines the responsibility to teach children the basic stories of the community's relationship with God and all that he has done for them. These days we might assume that the responsibility for this lies mainly with parents, rather than it being a role for the whole faith community. It is important for children to grow up knowing how God has worked in the lives of those around them. Each congregation should take this passage seriously, teaching Bible truths and showing how God has worked out these things in the lives of individuals and the whole church. This is both for their benefit and so that in turn they can pass it on to the next generation (see Psalm 78:4–8).

Children have a part to play in worship. Psalm 8:2 says:

'With praises from children and from tiny infants, you have built a fortress. It makes your

Bible verses

God's knowledge, care, love and concern for a child's growth is sometimes expressed in the Bible through clear statements:

> 'Children are a blessing and a gift from the Lord.' (Psalm 127:3)

> 'You are the one who put me together inside my mother's body.'
> (Psalm 139:13)

> 'Even before I was born, you had written in your book everything I would do.'
> (Psalm 139:16)

It is gleaned from God's ways of dealing with his people as a parent would a child:

> 'I took Israel by the arm and taught them to walk… I led them with kindness and with love, not with ropes. I held them close to me;
> I bent down to feed them.' (Hosea 11:3, 4)

> 'I took care of you in a thirsty desert. I fed you till you were satisfied.'
> (Hosea 13:5, 6)

It is proved by God's concern that children should know and understand what he has done for them in the past:

> 'Listen Israel! The Lord our God is the only true God! So love the Lord your God with all your heart, soul, and strength. Memorize his laws and tell them to your children over and over again. Talk about them all the time, whether you're at home or walking along the road or going to bed at night, or getting up in the morning. Write down copies and tie them to your wrists and foreheads to help you obey them. Write these laws on the door frames of your homes and on your town gates.' (Deuteronomy 6:4–9)

> 'Someday your children will ask, "Why did the Lord give us these laws and teachings?" Then you will answer: We were slaves of the king of Egypt, but the Lord used his great power and set us free. We saw him perform miracles and make horrible things happen to the king, his officials, and everyone else. The Lord rescued us from Egypt, so he could bring us into this land, as he had promised our ancestors. That's why the Lord our God demands that we obey his laws and worship him with fear and trembling. And if we do, he will protect us and help us be successful.' (Deuteronomy 6:20–25)

Chapter Link

There is much more on children in worship in chapter 8.

enemies silent, and all who turn against you are left speechless.'

As we seek to help children to praise God there are challenges for us about how we do that in ways beyond simply singing songs that are designated as 'suitable for children'!

Learning from what Jesus did

One of the best-known and important Bible passages about younger children comes in three of the four gospels. Matthew 19:13–15, Mark 10:13–16 and Luke 18:15–17 all record an incident where parents brought their children to Jesus for him to bless them. It is not clear what age these children were; depending on which translation of which gospel you read they are either 'children' or 'little children'. But some versions talk of Jesus taking the children into his arms to bless them, so unless he simply gave them each a hug, we might assume they were under the age of 8. Their exact age is unimportant: what matters here is that Jesus had time for them when his disciples – perhaps wanting to protect him – turned them away. Their parents saw the value of him blessing them and he did just that. He welcomed them and blessed them. In this, Jesus mirrored his father's care for these children whom he had known since they were in their mother's womb; today it is our task to care for children in ways that show God's love for them.

How does that challenge and shape our thinking and practice? On the opposite page there are questions to help you think about your church's baptism policy, and then further thinking about ways to encourage and help parents to bring their children to be blessed.

Learning from what Jesus said

Mark records Jesus as challenging the disciples to think about the way they accept God's kingdom, and telling them that they must do so as a little child. There are two important truths here. The first is about the way children receive things: offer a child a gift and they are excited and happy to receive it. An adult's response may involve suspicion, questioning why you are giving it, and what demands it will make of them, but a child – especially at this age – will be delighted with it and only inquisitive about what the gift is. That openness to all that they are offered demands integrity in the way we work with them, so that we do not abuse this wonderful quality. This willingness to accept all that they are offered means that we must never use 'bribes' to take spiritual steps. 'Become a Christian and you'll get a free Bible/book/box of chocolates' is not acceptable! The second truth, the fact that Jesus used a child as an example, means that another aspect of our Biblical basis for children's work should therefore be a willingness to learn from children, not just to assume that we will always teach them!

This was not the only time that Jesus used a child to teach his disciples. In Mark 9:33–37 and its parallel passages of Matthew 18:1–5 and Luke 9:46–48 he teaches them about serving others, reminding them that to welcome a child is to welcome him and 'the one who sent me' (Mark 9:37). Try to keep that in mind as your group arrives for your next session. Whether a child is noisy, boisterous, shy, a show-off, annoying, easy to work with, happy, miserable, clever – whatever they are like, welcome them and you will be welcoming God.

Baptism policy

It seems that many parents still want their children to be 'blessed'. Although the numbers of children being brought to churches for baptism has been declining for many years, there are still families with no regular church connection who want their child to be baptised. It may be because an older family member applies pressure, but parents themselves will often think this is the right thing to do simply because, in an almost superstitious way, they will take no chances! This challenges those churches that baptise children to think through their baptism policy:

- By baptising a child, is the church opening the child and their family to the grace of God?
- Is the church creating an opportunity to explain more about what they believe?
- Is the church colluding with a lack of understanding in such a way that parents assume this makes their child a Christian, and there is nothing more to do?
- How does the church prepare a family for baptism? And how do they support the family afterwards in bringing up their child to know Jesus?

There are challenges too for those churches that practise believer's baptism:

- Christian parents may want their child dedicated, but what about families who are on the edge of church and for whom that might be a step too far: what alternative can be offered to parents who want some kind of a blessing for their children?
- What can be offered to families who are not even church-goers, but who have some connection with the church, perhaps through a toddler group?
- How can either of these types of family be supported in bringing up their child to know Jesus?

In seeking the best for their children some parents will set aside their own uncertainties about God if they think he will look with favour on their young child. A vicar regularly involved with a parent and toddler group says, 'At the end of each session we sit together and I ask the parents to put their hands on their child and pray simply "God bless George", or whatever name. They won't refuse. They want the best for the child. Repeat that exercise regularly and within a few months they will be praying quite deep prayers for their children.'

Once a child has reached the age of five their parents are probably less likely to seek a blessing for them in the literal sense, but many who themselves have had even a minimal amount of Christian input in their own childhood will want their children to have every chance in life – including spiritually.

Chapter Link

Many churches are also thinking through the issues surrounding children and communion. These are considered in chapter 8.

Remembering that children represent him to us is especially vital at those points where their behaviour causes us frustration or annoyance!

In his gospel Matthew also records another time when Jesus taught his disciples through children. It seems probable that the 'little followers' of Matthew 18:6 are those who are humbly following Jesus, rather than children. But the warning should still apply: we must be vigilant about our words, actions and attitudes so that we do not cause children to sin. In practice that could mean all kinds of things, including:
- Ensuring that all who work with children in our church have a credible Christian lifestyle which does not deny the very truths they are teaching.
- Having all children's leaders meet together regularly to study the Bible passages that will be covered in forthcoming sessions to ensure they are taught accurately.
- Being fully prepared so that leaders are ready for the session. This means arriving early, having the room set up with everything to hand and being spiritually and emotionally ready. There are less likely to be discipline issues if we are self-disciplined!

There is one more important factor in the Biblical basis for working with children. We have already looked at how, in Matthew 21:14,15, Jesus was challenged by the chief priests and teachers of the law about his miracles and the fact that children were calling out to him as the Son of David. We know children will copy what they hear or see others say or do but it is also true that they can have a remarkably intuitive understanding of situations. We don't know if the children in Jesus' day were being intuitive or not but what is important is that we recognise the way young children are often instinctively aware of spiritual things.

We cannot prove this instinctive spiritual awareness but we do need to keep it in mind as we talk and work with children. We can sometimes spoil a child's understanding by telling them too much, or by not allowing them to tell us how they see things.

There are times when we need to remind ourselves that God can easily communicate with children without any adult involvement; our task is to nurture their awareness and help them discern what they are discovering about him.

Our final passage for consideration is Matthew 18:10–14. At first glance Jesus' story of a sheep being lost looks the same as that recorded in Luke 15:3–7, but the fundamental difference here is that Jesus is talking again about those who are 'little ones'. Again, it may be those who are 'little' in faith, but it could also mean little in years. The truth depicted here is that they are immensely precious to God, so much so that he does not want any to be lost. That alone should spur us on to work hard at what we do with children: to pray for them regularly, to pray for ourselves and our times with them and to do all we can to nurture belief and faith in them. Our time with them is not mere childminding, but is an opportunity to express God's love and care for them and to help them know him and grow in that knowledge.

So pause now to use the stories and guidance on the opposite page to pray for the children in your care – and for yourself as you relate to them.

Spiritual awareness

To tell the story of the last supper eaten by Jesus and his disciples, Lizzie sat her group round a table and gave everyone a chunk of fresh bread and a drink of blackcurrant juice. She was astonished at how quiet and almost reverent the children were, although she said nothing about the significance of the bread and wine until after they had eaten it.

A young child bent over her baby brother's cot and whispered to him, 'Tell me baby brother and remind me what God sounds like... I'm starting to forget'. Is that a 'sweet' story or reality?

A group of experienced children's leaders were asked what they thought about children being born with an inherent awareness of God which many then lost as they grew older because it was either nurtured out of them or not nurtured in them. The person leading the training session pointed to the opposite sides of the room they were in. 'Stand to my left if you think "yes, children are born with an innate awareness of God"... or stand to my right if you think "no". Stand somewhere in between if you're not sure'. The majority of the leaders stood to her left, fairly close to the wall.

Can you think of your own stories of children who have shown they are instinctively spiritually aware?

In 2001, Scripture Union International's children's network held a consultation entitled, 'Joining children on their spiritual journey'. Amongst the practical implications that emerged from the discussions were that those working with children should:

- Appreciate that all children have some spiritual sensitivity to God. The leader's task is to point them to the God of the Bible and to nurture them towards maturity in Christ.
- Be encouraged to trust the Holy Spirit to be the children's guide, with the adult leader being less prescriptive about the response a child should make at any given time.
- Take a 'step back' to allow each child to enter more fully the Bible text.
- Encourage children to respond to what God is doing in their lives.

Chapter 2 – The world of 5 to 7s

The physical world

When you are 5, 6 or 7 years old 'your world' is a strange and sometimes frustrating place. All too much of life happens well above your eye level! The average 5-year-old sees the world from just above the waist height of an average adult. And it all looks very different from there!

It is obvious why children of this age can become separated from their parents, if only momentarily, in crowded shops and supermarkets! But aside from the safety angle there are important issues about their height that we need to take into consideration.

- What is the height of tables and chairs where their group meets – is the furniture right for younger children?
- At what level are pictures or words projected? Can they be seen comfortably or do the children have to crane their necks?
- At what height do we display pictures either drawn by children or used to brighten rooms?
- What can a child see – and not see – when seated and when standing among a congregation in church? Is their view completely blocked?
- Signage – can they actually see, for example, which are the 'Ladies' and the 'Men's' toilets?
- Children are often told off for 'fiddling' with things that are on tables or shelves. Being at their eye level, it is unsurprising; we are looking above them and are less likely to notice them until the child picks them up. Do we provide things of interest for them, or tell them off for following their natural, inquisitive, instinct?
- Most importantly, do we tower above them or do we remember to bend, kneel or sit down to speak to them so that we can look them in the eye?

On the opposite page you will find the first of a series of practical exercises designed to help you understand better what it is like to be 5, 6 or 7. If you can, work through this page.

Children love colour, texture and variety in their world. These are still years of exploration, with great discoveries to be made. Objects are there to be picked up, turned over in the hands, studied in minute detail and then discarded or used for a game. Doors 'ask' to be opened and other people's houses 'need' to be inspected so that a child knows where it differs from their own. Having grown beyond the need to cling to dad's trousers or mum's skirt in a strange place, 5 to 7s find new venues are actually an adventure!

'We went to take a cake to a neighbour who wasn't very well, and she invited us in,' said Andy, father of 6-year-old Gary. 'As soon as we got in the house Gary's eyes were darting round all over the place to see what was different from our house. I was a bit worried what

Try this experiment!

If you happen to be reading this in a public place, such as on a bus or train, you may want to delay this exercise until later. On the other hand, it could be an interesting conversation starter...

If you can, stand up and take a good look round the room where you are reading this. Look at what is at your eye level, and especially at what surfaces are below your eye level.

If you can, kneel on the floor and move around the room on your knees. Or you can do this exercise by sitting on a chair positioned in different places around the room.

Look carefully again at everything, especially at what is at your eye level now.

Can you still see the same surfaces? What is above your eye level now?

What are you unable to see?

What does this teach you about the visual world of the five-year-old?

Lost in a crowd above your head

Similarly, try sitting down when there are lots of other people in the room who are standing and talking together.

What can you/can't you see?

How do you feel?

What does it make you want to do?

You will be experiencing something of the world of children aged five, six and seven. How might you use this experience when working with them?

he might say…'

'Whilst on holiday I went into the church on the island of Lindisfarne. It was busy with visitors including a girl about 5 years old and her family,' recalls Elaine, who leads a children's group in her church. 'This child was having a lovely time exploring the building, looking at hymn books, walking along different pews, checking behind curtains and even opening a cupboard door. And then her mother saw her, grabbed her by the arm and dragged her out of the church. Of course the child was upset and started to cry. I wondered what she would make of the whole episode later. Would she think, "I went to church once, but I got told off for just being me?"'

So the physical world of 5 to 7s is quite large, calling out to be investigated and discovered, to be played in and owned. But that may not be the case for all children of this age: some may be very content just to sit and do very little.

There is much talk in the media about obesity in children and links between that and excess of television and computer games and a lack of active play and exercise. For all kinds of reasons – from their own choice, to parental fear of 'stranger danger' – some children rarely play 'out', and if they do it will only be in their own enclosed area. Many are so hooked on computer or hand-held electronic games, and are taken to and from school by car, that they will rarely have any exercise. If we are working with children for only an hour or so each week we are not going to make a significant difference to their physical state, but where possible we should include active games, if only to show how much fun they can be! But, for example, a midweek children's club might include 15 minutes of 'mini gym' in their weekly programme, a series of exercises in the style of circuit training. We should certainly serve sugar-free squash, and perhaps fruit too, although when a particular church discussed serving 'healthy snacks' on a Sunday one of their children's leaders, who is a mother and a doctor, said, 'They get healthy stuff all week long – let them have biscuits as a treat on Sundays!'

The emotional world

For many children the years of being 5, 6 and 7 are very happy times. They have made it through the great life change of starting nursery and then school, and have settled into the new routines involved. Although they will still have times of extreme tiredness, frustration or temper that upset the emotional apple cart, they will generally be more stable than they were under the age of 5.

Their 'emotional world' will focus on four main groups of people:
• nuclear family
• extended family
• friends
• significant adults

Nuclear family

Stability in the nuclear family is crucial to a child's emotional state. This can be upset by

Joel's world

Joel is 6. He lives with his parents, older brother and younger sister. There is a two-year gap between each of the children, and the three get on well. Joel and his brother share a bedroom. They like playing with the same things much of the time. Except for those moments that almost all siblings have, when both want exactly the same toy, book or game at the same moment, this works well. Joel will also play happily with his sister, joining her in creating vans, cars, planes and the likes from dining chairs, using a circular table mat as a steering wheel.

He will play happily on his own too, with the toys that he is especially fond of, such as his sonic screwdriver. He enjoys card games and loves to play games on the computer. His lively sense of humour means that he enjoys stories, television programmes and films that make him laugh, and Joel loves reading jokes out of a book that the brothers share. You will find some of Joel's favourite jokes on the right hand pages of this chapter! Joel is especially fond of the family's Hornby railway and knows all about the rolling stock. His favourite engine is a 'Virgin', and he is innocently unaware of why his father encourages him to refer to it as a 'Virgin train'!

Many of these toys are long-term favourites, but ask Joel what is his favourite film or how he likes to spend Saturdays and his answer will often be shaped by his most recent enjoyable experience or the DVD he has just watched.

Joel looks up to his brother and will often try to emulate him in achievements. So, for example, he wanted a pair of football boots when his brother needed new ones, even though at the time he was not particularly keen on football. When asked what he would like as a birthday present, his older brother replied, 'A trumpet!' Asked the same question at the same time, Joel continued with the musical theme but said he would like a violin or a cello.

The family keeps chickens in their back garden and Joel is very attached to Amber, his hen, who lays more eggs than the others. If anyone coming to visit has not seen the hens the children will take them into the garden and introduce them to each one in turn. Joel thinks everyone should keep chickens!

(Continued on page 29)

change through either development (eg new sibling being born) or division (eg parental marriage break-up, long-term or severe illness, or death). Perhaps one of the most difficult things for a child of this age to deal with is the break-up of their parents' relationship and one or the other, or both of them, then creating a new family unit with a partner who also has children.

Jade's parents separated and her father moved in with his girlfriend. Jade would sometimes stay with them for a weekend and her class teacher could always tell when this was happening. Jade would become increasingly quiet as the weekend drew near and would be very tearful on the Friday morning as she said goodbye to her mother. Her father demanded that Jade referred to them as 'my daddy and his partner' but this upset Jade dreadfully and she would begin to sob as she said the words in class.

Roxanne loved visiting the homes of her friends when they had a new baby, but when her own younger brother was born she became moody and disruptive at both school and Rainbows. Although she helped to bath her brother and appeared to enjoy helping her parents she was actually very jealous and resented the attention that he got. It was only when she drew on her bedroom wall that her parents realised that they needed to deal with the problem, and began to give Roxanne the time and attention that she both wanted and needed.

Extended family

For many children the extended family has a particular importance. Some will rarely see their relations, who live at a distance, and so a visit for a holiday or special occasion is very memorable. Others will be brought up by their grandparents as much as by their parents, or be taken to and collected from school by them. Increasing numbers of children live in extended households either for cultural or financial reasons.

There is no doubt that today's children are more aware of family problems than children a generation or two ago. On the whole they understand more (perhaps because these issues are raised and discussed in television soaps) and pick up 'vibes' from adults. Sometimes they will make too much of a situation. A lady was driving her grandchildren home from school one day whilst their mother was at work and their father, who usually collected them, was away at a conference. He had rung her on her mobile phone but the signal was poor. At one point she shouted, 'Say that again, you're breaking up' and immediately her grandson in the back of the car said, 'If they're breaking up, can I live with Mum?'!

Friends

Friendships are important to children at this age but can easily be broken and mended in the space of a day! Some will make new friends as they start school but many will have friendships formed in toddler group or nursery. Some will know other children from an activity or out of school class, such as dance or judo, and children who grow up in church are likely to have friends from there. As you can read on pages 27 and 29, Joel has friends from church as well as school. As children grow older and are involved in more activities their circle of friends will most likely increase.

(Joel's world continued)

Joel goes to his local infants' school, a ten-minute walk from home. He says that he most enjoys asking questions of the teacher, but dislikes everything else! He found school very hard at the start and there were frequent mornings when he was unwilling to get up and get dressed. He also hated walking to school and developed delaying tactics so that sometimes they had to go by car. Those early days were tearful for both Joel and his mum. But despite saying he only likes asking questions he is now very happy at school and is getting on well.

Joel thinks deeply about things and takes in every detail of experiences, often not showing his reaction to important events until long after they are over. When he was 5 the family flew to France for a holiday and Joel, who loved playing with planes, was very quiet during the flight. He spent the time looking intently at everything, taking in every detail, and it was some days before he began to talk about the plane and all that he had seen.

At the age of 6 Joel has just 'got into clothes'. For some time he has wanted gel on his hair occasionally but now, suddenly, he is interested in what he wears as well. So he and his mum have recently had a shopping trip so that he could choose his own clothes rather than him wearing what she had bought for him. He liked this a lot!

As Joel's parents are very involved in their local church it is a familiar place to him and he has a number of friends there. He especially enjoys the end of the service, when all the children go out and play in the grounds at the side of the church, but he also enjoys the songs in church and the activities for his particular age group. He says Jesus is one of his heroes – along with Superman!

Joel will often ask deep questions of his parents as they eat a meal or while they are out in the car. Like many children of this age he has questions about death and has said several times that he would like to die and go to heaven, without necessarily understanding the implications of that.

On a recent trip in the neighbourhood Joel asked his mum, 'What kind of a house does God live in?' For a while they looked at the houses they were passing and finally decided that God's house must be bigger than all of them.

These are very important years for children to build strong friendships. Children who struggle to make friends at this age may find it even harder as they grow older. We need to give them all the help and support possible – but without being too manipulative! Jacqueline, who never found friendships easy in the early years at school, said later, 'Because we didn't get on well right at the start and I was with those same children all though Primary and Secondary school, I never had any really good friends.' As you work with this age group, think of what you can do to help them build secure and supportive friendships.

Significant adults

For many children there will also be one or two 'significant adults' who bring emotional stability to their world. They may be leaders of a uniformed organisation, childminders, regular babysitters, or leaders of children's activities. They will almost certainly include the child's class teacher from school. As a children's worker you are probably one! We should never underestimate the influence and impact we may have on a child's emotional world – nor overestimate it, either. To many children their church group leader or school teacher stands in a unique position of being both friend and 'grown-up' who can be told all kinds of 'secrets' and special things. We must have complete integrity in our dealings with children so that we never break that trust, nor damage the child through it.

The spiritual world

When we think about spirituality in children we often talk of them having a sense of 'awe and wonder'. If ever there was an age for that, it is the years when children are 5, 6 or 7. Light a candle as you quieten them for prayer and notice how they watch the flame. Show them tiny creatures through a magnifying glass as you talk about the wonder of God's creation and listen to their excited chatter as they take in every detail of the insect. Walk them through some of the wonderful Bible narratives of Jesus being born, of him feeding hungry people, of him being welcomed into Jerusalem, and include some of the sights, sounds, smells, tastes and textures associated with these encounters, and see their eyes widen with amazement!

The word 'spirituality' has a much wider meaning than just relating to the things of a particular faith or indeed of any faith. Children from a non-faith background will be just as aware of spiritual things as their friends whose families do have a particular belief, but they may not recognise them as being spiritual. In chapter 1 we considered the idea that children are born with an innate sensitivity to God. Depending on their family background and influences, that sensitivity may be nurtured out of a child and replaced by a different spirituality. It may simply not be nurtured in them and lost through neglect or it may be nurtured further by contact with Christian family or friends, church or activities run by Christians. Before a child starts school, their spiritual world will be almost exclusively influenced by home and family, and if others do have an influence it is likely that this will be through the choice of their parents (eg toddler group, church etc).

Once in school, however, children will pick up spiritual things there, whether taught directly or simply absorbed from the ethos of the school. At the end of her eldest child's first term in school a mother, herself a teacher, commented that it had been something of a shock to

Parents' influence on friendships

One 5-year-old said to another in the school playground, 'My mummy says I can't play with you because you're not a vegetarian!'

In a television interview two mothers admitted to the fact that whereas when they were young a child would say, 'Can my friend come round to play?' the approach now is for the parent to 'book' with another parent a play appointment for their children.

A newspaper article advised parents to look carefully at the other parents at the school gate and not to plan their child's friendships on the basis of 'Who would be a good friend for my child?' but on the basis of 'With which set of parents would we like to be friends?'!

Knock knock

Who's there?

Amen

Amen who?

Amen a lot of trouble...

Chapter Link

Chapter 6 includes information about leaders and the responsibility they have for the well-being of children.

realise that she no longer had control over her son's learning and knowledge. By the age of 5 a child's spiritual world will be increasingly influenced by the people they meet in school. In Britain, current government legislation requires schools to have a daily act of collective worship. The majority of these over a term should be 'wholly or mainly of a broadly Christian character', although (except in the case of Voluntary Aided, ie church schools) they should not be influenced by any particular denomination.

This presents a golden opportunity to influence and input into the spiritual world of children! Obviously the person who will do that most in school is a class teacher. However great the opportunity, this should not be anyone's prime motivation for entering the teaching profession! But it is clear that teachers have an enormous influence on the children in their care, and so a teacher who has a positive attitude towards the Bible can inspire children to love its stories too. When the Bible says, in James 3, 'Not all of you should be teachers' it is talking about teaching in church, but it reminds us that there are other ways to influence the spirituality of a school. You can do so as a non-teaching member of staff, such as a classroom assistant, secretary, caretaker or cleaner. Alternatively, you may want to consider the following ways to serve a school through which you can be 'salt and light' and make a more overt contribution to the spiritual life of the children and staff.

- As a school governor you would be part of the body that makes decisions about school policy and ethos, appoints staff and spends the budget.
- As a visitor leading collective worship you would have opportunity to teach God's truths and explain the message of the Bible, although this would need to be done with great care so that you were not saying, 'You must believe…' or even making the assumption of common thinking by saying, 'We believe…'. Rather, a Christian should work from the basis of 'Christians believe…' or 'The Bible says…'.
- As a visitor leading a lunchtime or after-school Christian club there is a little more freedom, since children who attend it are there voluntarily with parents' permission. Despite a club like this being extra to the curriculum and held at the head teacher's discretion you will still need to work with real integrity – but then all children's work requires that!
- As a volunteer listening to children read, coaching sport or music sessions, you would be in a position to encourage children and help them to feel good about themselves and their abilities.
- As a volunteer washing paint pots or doing other helpful tasks for busy teachers, baking cakes for staff to enjoy at the end of the week or sending a card with assurances of prayers before, or congratulations after, a school inspection, you would be showing God's love and care to the staff in ways that will flow over to the children.

There are numerous ways you can support a school and through that, also influence the spiritual world of children. The starting place – after prayer to be guided by God – is always with the head teacher, to find out what can be done and what would help them.

The following prayers are taken from Hey God...wot u up 2?, Salvation Army, 2006

Thank you God for helicopters and planes because they help to rescue people when they are lost. Amen.

Callum age 5

Dear God

Thank you for making the trees and flowers. They make our world beautiful and help our world to survive. Amen.

Lewis age 6

Dear God

Thank you for all the animals. Thank you for my hamster Harry. Please don't let people be bad to animals. Watch over them.

Rhegan age 6

Chapter Link

Chapter 8 looks in detail at children in the context of church and considers how church and its practices influence a child.

At this age children love stories, and the Bible is full of good ones! It is important to note here that a child's spiritual thinking will be influenced by the Bible passages they read or hear. Although the Old Testament is full of epic stories of adventure, it can be difficult for a young child to deal with the image of God that sometimes comes through them. Looked at objectively there is a lot of death and killing that makes no sense alongside God's commandment not to kill. It does seem strange that the story of Noah is included so readily in children's Bibles and so many people use it with younger children 'because they love stories with animals in them.' Whilst the animals in the ark were saved, the majority living on earth at that time were killed, and many a bright child, having asked, 'Why didn't God save all the animals when he flooded the earth?', has been unable to cope with the picture of God that emerges from the answer!

Children of this age have not lost their inherent inquisitiveness and our ability even just to allow them to ask questions, whether or not we can answer them, will build and strengthen children's spirituality. As we saw, Joel has lots of questions in his head which his parents encourage him to vocalise. They do not always know the answers but they are aware of the way his mind is working, the influences and experiences that have created those questions, and the impact that these are having on his world view and spirituality.

The school world

A large proportion of a child's average week is spent in school and, after their family it is the single most important influence on them at this age. Chapter 3 focuses on the school experience and how that affects 5 to 7s.

The social world

In Britain, children of this age are more likely to play together in each other's homes than simply playing 'out'. This is a huge change since their parents were children, and even more so since their grandparents were children, when even children this young might disappear off for hours at a time – perhaps with older siblings – to play in local parks or fields. However there is a growing recognition that this is harming children's social development and so there may be a gradual turnaround in this area.

A generation ago a child of this age would probably have celebrated their birthday with friends at home with a party consisting of games, 'a disco' (ie the family's own music on cassette tapes) and home-made food, including a home-made birthday cake. Some parents matched the number of guests to the age of the child (five for a fifth birthday). Today's child will often take a much larger group of friends to an activity such as bowling or an indoor adventure play area, followed by food on site or in a local pizza restaurant or similar. Each child will go home with a party bag full of small gifts that has cost a reasonable percentage of the value of the present they have brought for the birthday child! If the celebration is a party with games it may be run by a paid entertainer or include a magician or similar, the food served may be quite adult (rather than the jelly and ice cream of past generations!) and end with a birthday cake that was bought, not home-made. It is likely to be held at a hired venue

It is always enlightening to eavesdrop on the conversation between children of this age: to discover what they talk about together, and in what depth they discuss things.

Conversation One

Nicky and her sons, 8-year-old William and 6-year-old Matthew, had been for a walk with a friend and her dog. The boys adored Bouncer and loved to throw sticks for him to fetch. As she drove them home from the park Nicky listened in to their conversation.

Matthew I love Bouncer!

William   I love him more!

Matthew When I'm older I'm going to marry Bouncer!

William   You can't – he's a boy!

Nicky intervened at this moment to point out that the reason Matthew was unable to marry Bouncer was actually because he was a dog!

Conversation Two

One Sunday morning the 6 to 7s group in church were drawing or writing about things which they wanted to thank God for. Rhiannon was busy drawing her cousin who had been to stay over the recent holiday. Alex sat staring at his piece of paper, unable to think of anything.

'What's been good this week Alex?' asked one of the helpers. 'Have you been anywhere special or done anything you particularly enjoyed?'

Alex shook his head.

'What did you do last night?'

'Watched television,' said Alex, unenthusiastically.

'What did you watch?' asked the adult.

'Oh!' exclaimed Alex, 'Big Cat Diaries!' His eyes began to sparkle.

'I saw that too,' said Rhiannon, 'it was brilliant. I thought that cheetah cub would get killed!'

'Yes, said Alex, 'It was really scary. But I liked the leopards most. Did you see when the mother…'

And the two children were off, having a long discussion about the different animals shown on the programme and their favourite moments. The adult helper listened in and occasionally added her own comments. As other children heard the conversation they too joined in and it became clear that 'Big Cat Diaries' was a firm favourite with many of them. It featured in the prayer time at the end of the morning's session.

Chapter Link

Chapter 7 looks at the suitability of Bible narratives for younger children and at ways of teaching them.

rather than in a home, and the guest list may even include the child's entire class for fear of leaving anyone out. These are stressful and expensive times for parents, and the child whose birthday it is may not really enjoy the event as much as they had hoped. But amongst some families there is a feeling that 'it has to be done' because other parents will be critical if not, and that in turn may jeopardise their child's friendships!

How should adults talk with children? To some extent, the answer is 'the same way that we would talk with any of our peers'. Children do not like adults to talk down to them but will chat very happily about the right things if the conversation is pitched at the right level.

What conclusions would you draw from the two conversations on page 35? You might suggest that someone wanting to talk with children should:
• Find a topic that interests the children.
• Let them express their opinions – they certainly have them!
• Join in with the conversation that the children have without taking it over.
• Treat them respectfully as equals.
• Be genuinely interested in them and what they say.

The leisure world

The 5 to 7-year-olds' leisure world can include a whole range of activities:
• Hobbies – more so at the older end of the age range.
• Books – the amount read, and the titles selected, will vary according to children's reading level.
• TV – many children watch over two hours of television a day; a growing number have a TV in their bedroom and so may be watching considerably more than surveys suggest. Not only does this affect them as they may watch unsuitable programmes, but many watch TV late into the night and so are deprived of sleep, which has an impact on their academic work.
• Film – 2004 the Childwise Trends Report concluded that 24% of 5- to 6-year-olds visited the cinema once a fortnight or more often.
• Computer and game consoles – the above survey found that 77% of 5- to 6-year-olds had a games console at home.
• Play – at this age children will play with a huge variety of toys from the simplest doll to the most complex Lego systems.
• Sport – perhaps the most common are swimming, football, judo/karate that are seen as helpful in developing gross motor skills.
• Lessons – these will be mainly sport, dance or music.
• Clubs – Beavers, Rainbows, church weeknight clubs etc.

Perhaps what is most interesting here is that many children will be doing most of the above, not just one or two. If you are thinking of starting up a regular event for children then do find out first if they actually have room for anything further in their busy social and leisure diaries. Consider their parents too, who are dashing from place to place to get them from one event to another, often all on the same evening!

Sahithi
Aged 6

Emma
Aged 6

One of Joel's
favourite jokes

Knock knock

Who's there?

Boxer

Boxer who?

Box of chocolates

The world of imagination

The imagination of most 5- to 7-year-olds is a wonderful thing! Without hesitation most of them will invent games, situations and whole 'worlds' in which to play. These often involve toys or simple equipment, and possibly created and invisible characters. As an adult it is an enormous privilege to be invited into their imaginary world. Of course it may also be complex and confusing!

One mother tells of her daughter aged 5 having an imaginary friend called Puffalump. In reality Puffalump was a cloth pig but in the mind of this child he took on a live form. Even the girl's brother, two years older, played along with this and Puffalump was in their fantasy world for about three years. If he did not literally go away with the family on a day trip, it did not matter for, as the mother says, 'His car was faster than ours and he would suddenly appear. "Oh, there he goes!" one of them would call out at some stage of a journey!' Puffalump was even known to baptise people with a water pistol!

As we will consider in chapter 7, we will do well to harness these vivid imaginations and make the best use of them when it comes to talking about God! But it is not always easy, as children at this age see no difference between magic (ie illusion or false) and miracle (ie of God and therefore true). So Joel's question for Jesus of, 'How do you do your stuff?' was echoed by his brother, just 8, as 'How do you do your tricks?' Some would say that we should not use narratives of miracles with children at this age. It is good to think it all through, and to consider how you will explain the difference to children who confuse the two. There are some suggestions for this on page 37.

The cultural world

Today's 5-, 6- and 7-year-olds have more power as consumers than any generation before them! On average they receive more pocket money, have more idea of what to spend it on and are also targeted much more by advertisers who recognise that they, not just their parents, will decide what toys and other goods they buy.

They are equally targeted in terms of fashion, with the emphasis on them being 'miniature adults' rather than children. Popular adult fashions are likely to be popular with children too. You can virtually work out the age of a girl by the colour of her clothes: in pink, she will be 5 or 6, whereas by the age of 7 she will have moved on to lilac. Pistachio green is also favoured, and possibly purple in winter; in fact any fashionable colour worn by her mother will probably appeal. For boys, the fashion is more likely to be greens, khakis and browns, with the emphasis being on logos rather than pictures adorning the front of T-shirts. For them, as well as for girls, hair now matters – many will want the products used by their fathers, and it will be important for them to be like others among their friends.

Today's children are usually in school with children from a wider cross section of the community than previous generations, both in terms of faith, ethnicity and economics (although the latter may not apply if they do not attend a school in the state sector). They will

Magic or miracle?

Water turned into wine…. 5,000 men fed from five loaves and two fish, with 12 baskets full of leftovers… a blue handkerchief is pushed into an empty bag but a red one is pulled out… Which is magic and which is miracle in the eyes of a child? And does it matter if they see no difference?

Magic can always be explained. Very few magicians will actually tell you the secret of their tricks, but there will be an explanation. So, for example, the 'empty' bag into which a blue handkerchief is placed will have within it a separate compartment which secretes the red handkerchief until it is needed. A simple movement of the hand holding the bag will close one and open the other, so that the bag can then be turned inside out and still appear to be empty. Ask among your church congregation if someone can perform a simple magic trick and then explain it to the children to help them understand that tricks – even the most elaborate ones – can be explained.

Magicians are simply creating illusions: making their audience see or believe something that is not actually true. So the aim of a magic trick is just that: to 'trick' the audience whilst entertaining them, and to make the magician look clever.

Miracles, however, have no explanation other than that God is powerful and has authority over his creation. Jesus worked miracles in order to do two things: to benefit those who were in need, thereby showing God's love for them, and as signs that the kingdom of God was at hand.

During his trial, Jesus was sent to King Herod.

'For a long time Herod had wanted to see Jesus and was very happy because he finally had this chance. He had heard many things about Jesus and hoped to see him work a miracle.' Luke 23:8

If Jesus had worked a miracle, would Herod have sent word to Pilate to spare his life? It was unlikely anyway that Herod would have recognised Jesus as God's son, but Jesus did not work a miracle; he never used his power to save himself. Instead he used it to meet a need and to help others to see truth.

Here are some helpful things to keep in mind as you explain the difference between magic and miracle:

Magic tricks have to be learnt and they can always be explained and done by someone else. There is no explanation for Jesus' miracles other than that, as God's son, he has power.

Tricks are ultimately about making the magician look clever. Miracles are about meeting a need and showing that God's kingdom is present.

Avoid using the word 'performed' about Jesus and miracles as it has connotations of a staged act; try to say that he worked miracles instead. When referring to Jesus, never use the words 'magic', 'tricks', 'spell-bound', 'secret words' or any phrase that would relate more comfortably to Harry Potter than to Jesus.

usually travel more widely than their parents did, being more likely to have their first holiday abroad at this stage of their lives. The world is a much bigger place for them than it ever was for their ancestors.

The outside world

For all this early maturity and fashion consciousness, for all their travel and breadth of experience, today's 5-, 6- and 7-year-olds often live in very controlled environments. Many have allergies or asthma and pick up tummy bugs quickly; some would say this is due to their limited exposure to the normal world and an over-emphasis on their environment being 'squeaky clean'. Most are not allowed to play out unless accompanied by an adult. Instead they are constantly warned about 'stranger danger'. Many will be aware of the sad and distressing things that happen in the world; a great number will watch children's news programmes and so be all too aware that other children of their age face abuse, neglect, abduction, illness and death. Little wonder their parents try to protect them from these things.

Many will only enjoy indoor play. Indeed one teacher has spoken of teaching boys who are so used to playing computer and electronic games that they will only answer when spoken to from behind! One uncle describes giving his nephews, then aged 8 and 6, a rugby ball. Normally they never played together but spent time on their individual pocket electronic games. He was fascinated by their reaction to his gift and delighted that at long last they wanted to be out in the garden running and throwing their new toy. They saw it as a real novelty!

We need to keep up with this world, to understand it, to enter it as and when appropriate. We do well to watch their TV programmes regularly, to scan through their books from time to time and to chat with them whenever we can. We also need to look at it from a distance so that we can better help them to know and meet the God who created them and placed them in it, the God who loves them dearly.

Every Child Matters

As Christians working with children this is a truth that we hold dear, but in this case it refers to a Green Paper published by the United Kingdom Government in 2003. The Paper has five main outcomes that now underpin work with children in all aspects of education and community life.

A number of issues arise from Every Child Matters. For example, in order for every child to achieve economic well-being, child poverty has been tackled by way of making it possible for parents to earn more money. The Extended Schools Initiative offers parents the option of childcare either side of school time, so making it easier for them to work longer hours. It has a number of other aspects to do with better use of school facilities by the wider community, but one of its basic foundations is lifting more families from poverty.

As we work with children we need to keep these outcomes in mind. We are not likely to match

Questions Joel would ask Jesus if he came to his house.

'If you've got the whole world in your hands, what do you do when you want to drink a cup of tea?'

'How do you do your stuff?'

'What's it like sitting on a cloud?'

all of them, but they raise questions for us to consider as we plan and run our programmes.

- Safe: is what we do safe for children and well-organised?
- Healthy: how and what can we build into our programmes to enable children to be and stay healthy? Do we have policies, for example, about infectious diseases and how we will deal with any child affected by say chicken pox or German measles? Do we have a qualified first aider on our team, or does someone need to train in this?
- Enjoy and achieve: does our programme build the confidence and self-esteem of the children so that each knows when they have done well, regardless of whether their 'best' measures up to that of another child?
- Economic well-being: how do we cater for those families at the lower end of the financial spectrum? In terms of our approach to them, do we treat all children equally, regardless of their family's financial situation?
- Positive contribution: to what extent does our church allow children to contribute to the life of its community? There is more on this in chapter 8.

The five outcomes of Every Child Matters are that every child should be able to:

- Be healthy.
- Stay safe.
- Enjoy and achieve.
- Make a positive contribution.
- Achieve economic well-being.

With the order changed a little, they are commonly remembered by the acronym SHEEP:

- Safe
- Healthy
- Enjoy and achieve
- Economic well-being
- Positive contribution

For more information visit **www.everychildmatters.gov.uk**

See also *Top Tips on Demonstrating Every child matters* (Published by SU, July 2008)

Chapter Link

Chapter 6 looks at child protection and safety issues.

Chapter 3 – The development of 5 to 7s

Although the education system has traditionally separated primary children into infants and juniors there is a huge difference between an average child who has just turned 5 from the one who is about to celebrate their eighth birthday, even without taking into consideration those children who may have Special Educational Needs.

Physical development

In general there are two strands of physical development in young children which need to be considered when planning a range of activities: gross motor skills which are the main movements of the body and the limbs; and fine motor skills which are the more refined and specific movements made, for example, by our fingers and hands.

Gross motor skills

Most gross development occurs within the first five or six years of a child's life.

By the age of 6 most children will be able to:

- Walk
- Run
- Jump
- Skip
- Hop
- Balance
- Throw – but not always accurately
- Catch – with varying degrees of success

After the age of 6 there is a general qualitative improvement in the control children may have over these movements, but the majority will have mastered most of them by then. However, there are still children within the 5 to 7 age range who may find some of these activities more difficult than their peers. A quick assessment of a child's gross motor skills can be made by seeing who can skip. Children who find skipping (from one foot to another, not the sort with a rope) difficult are generally weaker in terms of gross motor skills and this should be considered when planning games which involve physical activity.

It goes without saying that a child who feels that they cannot do what their peers can may feel less confident about themselves. We need to make sure that all children feel emotionally valued and secure even if they lag behind their friends and siblings (who may be younger) in this or other respects. An additional consideration is that many more children take much less physical exercise for a whole range of reasons than their counterparts a generation ago.

Action games

a) Traditional Games

- Heads, Shoulders, Knees and Toes
- The Hokey Cokey
- Row, Row, Row your boat
- If you're happy and you know it
- The Grand Old Duke of York
- Simon Says

b) More Active Games for larger spaces

Traffic Lights. Have one green, one red and one yellow card. Hold up each card in turn. Children need to move as directed by the cards and the adult's instructions – red for stop, yellow for turn, green for running without bumping into anyone.

Bean Game. An adult shouts out different bean names and children follow the instructions: frozen bean – stay still; runner bean – run on the spot; jumping bean – jump on the spot; baked bean – crouch into bean shape on the floor and broad bean – children make as wide a shape as possible with their legs and arms.

Fruit Bowl. Children stand in a circle. Go round and give each child a fruit name (orange, apple, banana – about three names works best). An adult calls out one of the fruit names and all the children who are 'oranges', for example, run across the circle and swap place with another 'orange' When 'fruit bowl' is called, all the children swap places.

Noah's Ark. Children stand in a circle. Five animal names are chosen and actions are taught by the adult (eg a kangaroo jumping, a frog crouching and then hopping, a penguin standing with feet together, arms by sides and bent at the waist). Five children are picked to be the animals. They remain in the circle until chosen by the adult, when they move into the centre of the circle and begin their action for everybody to copy. A sixth child can be Noah, who calls, 'Quick animals, into the ark' and all the children walk around in the circle.

Pass the beanbags (or similar items). Children stand in a circle. An adult gives out several beanbags at random. Music is started and the beanbags are passed around in the same direction. When the music stops, the children holding the beanbags have to perform named actions for a count of 10. The music is then started again, so that other children can have a turn.

Fine motor skills

In contrast to the lack of any major change in gross motor skills there is a huge development in fine motor coordination between the ages of 5 and 8. This is immediately apparent when looking at children's drawing and handwriting.

In general it is difficult to make statements about when children achieve good fine motor control as some 5-year-olds may be able to draw pictures with considerable detail whereas there are older children whose drawings may be quite immature. However, research seems to indicate that there is often (although not always) a link between those children who are slower at developing gross motor skills and their fine motor development. It is also apparent that most girls are about 18 months ahead of boys when it comes to the quality of their colouring, drawing, painting, writing and manipulating small objects or making models with plasticene.

Social and emotional development

Healthy social and emotional development is vitally important to ensure the happiness of the 5- to 7-year-old child. If children are unable to interact with their families or friends who are more obviously and concretely 'real' they will find it much harder to develop a relationship with a less concrete and more abstract God. A happy and contented child will be more receptive to learning and experiencing new things.

In today's world there are many more pressures being put upon young children than before and they are less innocent and naïve than the children of even a generation ago.

Some of the ways in which young children may feel pressured are:

Different family situations
It is a sad fact that an increasing number of children come from homes which lack stability for one reason or another.
- There are more single parent families, usually mothers, trying to bring up children on limited financial resources or with little time for their children as they need to go out to work.
- There are also more families where the parents may each be divorced and bring children of their own into the family.
- Additional children from these new relationships may also be born, complicating the family situation further.
- There are more families who – for a variety of reasons – have two working parents, which means that children may spend more time with a childminder or nanny during the day.
- In a few cases children may live in a family where both parents are the same sex.
- Increasingly geographical mobility means that most parents are less likely to have support from nearby family members such as grandparents, aunts and uncles who can be role models and offer valuable support and stability within children's lives.

Most 5-year-olds can:

- Begin to write their name.
- Draw or paint a picture of themselves or others. This usually consists of a face, possibly with a body and arms and legs. (In more basic drawings the arms may come straight from the face with no body.) When drawing their family or others they usually represent themselves as the largest person.
- Colour in a picture roughly, without necessarily choosing appropriate colours or taking much consideration of the lines
- Make things with play dough, but find it harder to manipulate plasticine or clay which is much harder and requires more upper arm strength.

Most 7-year-olds can:

- Write at some length. Their sentences will not always be punctuated correctly but they will usually make sense! The words will be spaced out and the spelling will vary enormously from child to child. Longer, more tricky words will be spelt phonetically so it is usually possible to read what a child has written by sounding it out!
- Draw or paint a picture of themselves with some accuracy. In addition to the basic face and limbs a body is nearly always present, often with clothes. There is more refinement of facial features with hair, ears, eyebrows and eyelashes, teeth and nostrils. Fingers and feet will probably be present although there may not be five digits on each hand or foot!
- Colouring will be much more controlled. Most children will have chosen appropriate colours, eg blue for the sky and green for grass, and will have made some attempt to stay within the boundaries of the lines, perhaps by colouring around the edges of the shapes before filling in the rest of them neatly.
- Be able to make recognisable models with clay or plasticine, using a range of simple tools to add more detail and joining more than one piece together.

Interestingly, children from ethnic minority groups may have more support, partly from extended families, but also from within their own community.

- The increasing fluidity of society means that we cannot take for granted that each child has a mother and father at home. Although there are many families like those mentioned above where parents succeed in providing a loving, caring environment for their children there is inevitably some disruption. This may cause children to feel very unsettled, in the same way that any form of change, like the birth of a new baby, for example, will affect them. Fortunately young children are very resilient and adaptable, but we need to be sensitive to their individual needs at any given time
- It is not only children from families with very little financial means who may lack stability within their family life. There are some children from financially secure backgrounds who see very little of their busy parents. These children may have every material need met, but lack the security of a loving and communicative relationship.

Academic expectations

Most children of 7 are aware that their academic ability will be assessed by their teachers, sometimes due to overanxious parents who try to coach them to do well in reading, writing and numeracy tests. Some parents not only buy workbooks for children to complete at home, they may even send their children to a tutor to try and improve their academic performance.

Expectations in other areas of their lives

There is a huge range of extra-curricular activities available for children, some of which make considerable demands upon them. These include after-school clubs, traditional children's groups such as Rainbows and Beavers and music, dance and sports lessons. Some children may have as many as 12 additional activities each week in non-school time! Partly this is due to fear amongst parents which prevents them allowing their children to play outside unsupervised but it means that children sometimes find it very difficult to generate their own entertainment without the intervention of an adult. It also means that children have little time to get bored and just be or think which may have repercussions for their spiritual development.

Television programmes and other media

Many children are more likely to be exposed to a greater range of programmes on television than they would have been in the past, partly because their busy parents may be juggling a job as well as running a home and they may be inclined to use the television or DVDs and videos to 'child mind' while they get on with something else after a hard day at work. Whilst a nine o'clock watershed is enforced by broadcasters to prevent children from viewing scenes of an explicitly violent or sexual nature, not all young children are in bed by that time and it is certainly not unusual to find that many of our 5 to 7s have been watching programmes like Eastenders with its obviously adult content. This is partly because some parents feel guilty about not spending enough time with their children and – confusing the quantity of time with the much talked about quality time – they keep their children up later than would have been the case some years ago. Inevitably the content of these programmes has an impact on young children. Quite aside from the language being used it is evident that

Finger rhymes and games

a) Traditional finger rhymes and games

- One finger, one thumb
- The Wheels on the Bus
- Head, Shoulders, Knees and Toes
- My Father Went to Sea, Sea, Sea
- Wind the Bobbin Up
- Ten in the Bed
- This Old Man

b) Finger play for improved fine motor skills

- Have strips of crepe bandage, lay them on a table and get the children to gather them by 'walking' their fingers and gathering the bandage into their hands.
- Children screw up pieces of newspaper into balls. These can be patted along the floor in a race or children can throw them onto a simple target.
- Roll play dough or plasticine into long sausage shapes and then form into snail-like spirals.
- Threading beads onto long pieces of plastic thread (these are available very cheaply).
- Put tips of little fingers of both hands together. Then move tips of ring fingers, middle fingers, index fingers and finally thumbs together. Reverse the order and see how fast you can get repeating these actions.

children are more aware of sexual issues, even though they do not quite understand them. Computer games and television have had a big impact on the way children play. Children mimic the behaviour of characters from television and act out the games which they play on game consoles in the same way that they would pretend to be mummies, daddies, doctors, nurses and teachers. For some children the majority of time at home is spent playing these games, some of which are of a violent nature. This is particularly the case with boys, for some of whom the world of computer games may be more real than their everyday lives. Girls tend to be less inclined to play computer games although they are still heavily influenced by television.

Being different from their friends

This has always been an issue, but in today's image-conscious world it seems even more important to children that they have the latest toys, clothes and food to eat. Advertising on television has a huge role to play in causing material awareness among children so that they are more likely to feel either superior or inferior to their peers.

Any of these factors may be at work in affecting the social and emotional life of young children. In particular it is worth asking oneself, in the case of a child whose behaviour seems unusual or difficult, if any of these may be the cause of the child's unhappiness. In some rare cases it may even be necessary to consider our roles in terms of child protection.

Intellectual or Cognitive Development

Children make huge strides intellectually between the ages of 5 and 7, which is what makes them so rewarding to work with, if at times challenging too! The intellectual abilities of a 5-year-old are very different from those of a child about to turn 8.

Recently the education system has changed in England and Wales and is based on Key Stages. As children move into Key Stage 1 (Years 1 and 2 where children turn 6 and then 7 respectively) the curriculum becomes much more structured and consequently demanding, with an emphasis on acquiring important basic skills, such as reading, writing and an understanding of basic mathematics. When 7-year-olds leave infant school they move into Key Stage 2 (Years 3 to 6) where it is assumed that most average children will have attained a reasonable standard of literacy and numeracy and there is a much greater emphasis on using these skills to gain more subject knowledge. Northern Ireland has Key Stages but there is no reception class so 7- to 8-year-olds are in Year 4 (the equivalent of Year 3 in England and Wales). In Scotland there are no Key Stages, just Primary and Secondary. The year numbers follow the same as England apart from there being an extra primary year – Year 7 for 11 to 12-year-olds.

How do children develop intellectually between the ages of 5 and 7?

Academics agree that intellectual development goes hand in hand with children's language development. Whilst most children aged 5 have a reasonably extensive vocabulary, regardless of social background, the acquisition of language isn't finished by the age of 5.

A mother was preparing pancakes for her sons, Kevin 5, and Ryan 3. The boys began to argue over who would get the first pancake. Their mother saw the opportunity for a moral lesson.

'If Jesus were sitting here, he would say, "Let my brother have the first pancake, I can wait."

Kevin turned to his younger brother and said, 'Ryan, you be Jesus!'

A mum invited some people for a family meal. At the table, she turned to their six-year-old daughter and said, 'Would you like to say the blessing?'

'I wouldn't know what to say,' the girl replied.

'Just say what you hear Mommy say,' the wife answered.

The daughter bowed her head and said, 'Lord, why on earth did I invite all these people to dinner?'

We were talking at breakfast time with Tom (5) about heaven and what it will be like. Tom was saying about all the things he knew and we were putting in bits too. Suddenly he looked all excited and asked, 'Mummy, where are the toilets in heaven?'

When thinking about poverty Ann (6) said, 'I don't think Father Christmas goes to Uganda'

When Ella (5) came home from her first day at school she was asked, 'How did you get on?'

'Fine,' came the reply, 'but I haven't learnt anything yet.'

Most children of 5 still, for example, talk about 'sheeps' instead of 'sheep' and tell people they 'cutted' the pictures out! This is because they have learnt some of the rules of language (in this case, plurals and the past tense) but don't know the exceptions. Similarly they don't understand that words may have different meanings.

For example in the book *Cider with Rosie* Laurie Lee recalls his first day of school and being told by the teacher to 'wait here for the present'. At the end of the day he is unhappy to discover that he is not to receive a gift! A more recent example is from a family who were sitting round the dinner table when the older brother (nearly 8) told a joke. 'What's green and goes camping?' His younger sister replied she didn't know and the brother replied, 'A Brussels' scout' at which both children burst into loud laughter. The younger sister, not wanting to be left out, asked her brother the same joke. He didn't know so she gleefully told him, 'A broccoli'. Of course, the older child protested loudly that this didn't make sense, but to the younger child it made perfect sense: she had used exactly the same question and had answered it with the name of a green vegetable, just as she assumed her brother had, not realising that he understood the very careful play on words.

The reason this is so is that younger children (and also those with special educational needs) take things very literally. They understand life from their experiences in the concrete world first and foremost. Later they become able to understand that these 'real' objects can be represented on paper in drawings and pictures and photographs. Finally the child is able to understand more abstract ideas. This is critical when we are talking to children about God. If we present God merely as a historical character from a book (and many young children find the whole concept of time difficult to understand) rather than a living being with whom we can enjoy a relationship, then at best he will always appear to be a distant person rather than a constant, loving and ever-present friend.

Moral development

Very young children are extremely egocentric! You have only to traipse around the aisles of the supermarket to hear small children demanding something from their harassed-looking parents. In many ways this may be simply a reflection of the need to survive rather than a way of seeking attention. Children of this age tend to play alongside one another rather than with each other. However, between the ages of 3 and 6, children start to interact with each other more and begin to develop a rudimentary understanding of morality as a result. Their morality, however, tends to be very black and white and, just as in the case of language development, they do not understand different degrees of right and wrong and take things extremely literally.

For example, a family of two children (8 and 5) were having dinner with one of their friends when the father asked if the visitor liked red cabbage, as that was supposedly the 'secret ingredient' in the meal! The older child protested that there couldn't possibly be red cabbage in the meal as the father himself did not enjoy red cabbage, but the younger child was outraged at her father's suggestion and said that he was lying. The father explained that it was just a joke but the younger child protested vehemently that it wasn't a joke, saying, 'No,

Compare the handwriting of two 6-year-olds.

First we ...
went onthe coach.
Registr.
allowed

First we dune the
ragster. then
we mrs lamb
said elat

it's a lie, really!'.

Similarly, a young girl of 5, told the story of a child who broke one cup intentionally and another who broke several accidentally, thought the latter was worse 'because it's more cups'. Her slightly older brother, however, thought the former was worse because it was done 'on purpose'. There is a big shift here, again, between the literalism of the younger child and the more considered understanding of a child who is almost 8. This is something to be aware of as we deal with complex issues of right and wrong when helping our 5 to 7s learn about God.

Faith development

We know a great deal about how children develop physically, intellectually, emotionally and socially but the evidence for how faith develops is less clear-cut. A number of theories have been put forward and some about these early years of children's lives are summarised here.

Bruce Powers suggests that faith – an expression of trust in the unknown – is therefore an interpretation of the way people have experienced life. He writes about how, before the age of 7, his parents and Sunday School teachers enabled him to feel love and security. It was not what they taught him that showed this, but through the care and love they had for him. (Bruce Powers, *Growing Faith*, Nashville, Broadman Press, 1982)

In his book *Will our Children Have Faith?*(New York, Seabury Press, 1976) John Westerhoff III wrote about the impact of early years' experiences on faith, suggesting that we receive the faith that is important to those who nurture us. In this work he likened the growth of faith to the rings of a tree trunk, and described this innermost circle as 'experienced faith'.

Both James Fowler (*Weaving the New Creation*, New York, Harper Collins, 1991), and Dr. Larry Stephens (*Building a Foundation For Your Child's Faith*, Zondervan, 1996) commented on the fact that in pre-school years, parents or other adults to whom a child is emotionally attached, shape their understanding of God by the way they act. So by the age of 7, a child is still deeply influenced by parents or carers, but is also beginning to be influenced by others, eg teachers.

Psychologist Gordon Allport describes the first stage of faith as being 'raw credulity', where the child accepts everything they are told. (*Journal of Psychology and Theology*, 1997, vol 25, no 1, 53)

Whether or not we accept any or all of these theories, they give us useful points to help us enable children to develop faith in healthy ways.

If a child has a positive early experience of church – for example, beginning with a warm, carpeted crèche and kind people – and we tell them that God is loving and caring, their experience matches this truth. That gives them the right start to develop faith in an accurately modelled God. As one wise grandmother has described it, 'Our evangelism in these early

Most 5-year-olds are able to:

- Talk about things of immediate interest to them.
- Say whether they like something or not.
- Talk about what they see in a book or a picture.
- Recognise words, letters and numbers which have some significance to them.
- Count, add and subtract using real objects.
- Say how they are feeling.

Most 6-year-olds are able to:

- Talk about things both of immediate interest to them and also comment on things which may be of interest to others.
- Say whether they like something or not and possibly why.
- Read a simple text which uses many of the common words like 'cat' which are phonetically regular, and answer straightforward questions about it such as being able to say whether the cat is black or ginger.
- Recognise a number by a pattern, for example on a dice or the way objects are grouped in an illustration. When adding up they can keep one number in their head and count on instead of starting back at zero each time.
- Understand that others have feelings as well and that they may not be the same as the feelings they have at that time.

Most 7-year-olds are able to:

- Talk about something in a way which takes account of the needs of the listeners. For example, they use more formal language when explaining something to a group as opposed to being more chatty and informal with their best friend.
- Say whether they like something or not, giving some reasons for their opinion.
- Read more complex texts with irregular words and understand more fully what they have read. By the time the child is almost 8 many children (especially from more literate backgrounds) will be able to grasp meanings which may only be inferred in the text.
- Have a mental image of many abstract mathematical concepts, such as shapes and numbers and be able to calculate mentally using recall of number bonds.

years is through smiles, such as when a young child gazes at us in church from the security of their parent's shoulder.' Being accepted and loved by those who represent God enables a child to go on experiencing God as loving.

Taking on board the fact that young children accept things without question, we must take great care not to teach them anything that they will later need to 'unlearn'. This might include particular denominational beliefs (eg about practices, such as baptism) or Bible truths that we consider are too hard for them to understand, so we water them down to make them acceptable (eg what happens to people when they die). It could also be very simple things, such as the fact that to aid their concentration we often suggest children close their eyes and put their hands together when they pray. There is nothing wrong with that, but they need to know too that God answers prayers that are prayed with unclasped hands and open eyes! We should not sell them short by telling half truths; it is not enough to say that following Jesus is about always having a friend there in the tough times as well as the good times. Christian discipleship is about obedience, about responsibilities, as well as about rights. We need the skills to explain it at the right level for children. For example, to follow Jesus means trying to be like him; perhaps trying to love even those who tease us, or telling the truth even if we get into trouble for it, as well as having Jesus with us at all times, whether things are tough or easy.

The key thing, of course, is to allow faith to develop. Faith development theories recognise that if the right conditions for growth and nurture of faith have not been available, it is possible to be still at the 'experienced' stage of early years faith even when an adult. But generally faith develops as the child develops, and the faith that a child has at the age of 5, based on their experiences of love from significant adults, needs to grow to the faith of a 7-year-old that will be more focused on the values and interests of their friends. At this age, the idea of being one of Jesus' friends is very appealing. We must nurture that with care but never abuse their openness to good things. For more on this read *Top Tips on Encouraging Faith to Grow* (SU 2008).

So how do we help 5 to 7s learn about God?
All this has huge implications for those of us teaching children, between the ages of 5 and 7, about God. An 'average' 5-year-old is developmentally quite different from an 'average' 7-year-old, without even taking into consideration those children who may be either exceptionally advanced in one or more of the areas above or have special educational needs. Understanding how young children grow and develop enables us to look at each child as an individual, in the same way that God sees them, while at the same time being able to place them on a continuum of development which will help us to pitch our work at an appropriate level, so the children are able to enjoy being in God's presence more and learn more about him. However, by considering if we have more 5-year-olds than 7-year-olds or some children with learning difficulties within our groups, we may change the activities and expectations of our sessions. It may be necessary for those of us who work with children each Sunday to change the way we work throughout the academic year as younger children join the group or older ones leave. For example, when we have a lot of younger children we

Both these pictures were drawn by 6-year-olds.
Notice the difference of artwork from children of the same age

may provide more play and practical activities which do not require filling in their name and colouring.

It is also, perhaps, worth taking our example about how to help these young children learn about God from God himself. The Israelites of the Old Testament struggled to understand the very nature of God, who appeared distant and so holy that they could not approach him, aside from one or two very special occasions each year when the priests went into the temple to present sacrifices to him. God, however, then sent himself in the form of his son, Jesus, so that people could understand what he was like, so that they could have a relationship with him.

In the same way God can appear very abstract for our 'literal' 5 to 7s unless we make sure they understand that God is a person with whom they can enjoy a relationship in the same way they have relationships with their friends, family and those who work with them. We need to move on from the idea of Sunday 'schools' where children come to be 'taught' about God and encourage children to learn about and develop their relationship with God. One of the main ways to do this is to develop our own relationships with the children themselves.

How can current educational practice help us?

The role of play in learning

Whilst most of us tend to assume that play is more relevant in working with the under 5s, 5- to 7-year-olds still need to experience play activities. Indeed arguably there is a need for play amongst older children, too, but with the advent of so many supervised activities after school, children seem to have lost some of the ability to play with their peers.

In many countries, particularly Scandinavia where literacy levels are extremely high, children do not learn to read and write until they are almost 7, as research has indicated they learn more through structured play activities than more formal teaching. This would mean that only the oldest children within the 5 to 7 age group would have experienced school as we know it.

Recently in the UK there has been a move away from more traditional teaching and learning with the development of the Foundation Stage, which covers children in Nursery and Reception (3- to 5-year-olds). Whilst some more formal group sessions take place, children of this age are encouraged to talk, plan, question, experiment, repeat and reflect when they play at a range of carefully thought out play activities. These help them learn with enjoyment, and in a way which is challenging and helps them make sense of their world.

Play also enables children to relax and express themselves in a way that they are not able to do when they learn more formally. This, in turn, may help children to share things which are of importance to them and can be an additional bonus in developing our relationship with them, which is the key to developing young children's relationship with a living God.

Educational acronyms

ADD	Attention Deficit Disorder
ADHD	Attention Deficit and Hyperactivity Disorder
ASD	Autistic Spectrum Disorder
BDA	British Dyslexia Association
DfCSF	Department for Children, Schools and families, formely the DfES
EBD	Emotional and Behavioural Difficulties
ELG	Early Learning Goals: the expected standards children should reach in various areas by the end of the Foundation Stage
EAL	Children for whom English is not their mother tongue but an additional language
HI	Hearing Impaired
IEP	Individual Education Plan: a specific set of targets set in Primary School, usually related to learning or behavioural difficulties
KS1	Key Stage 1: Years 1(5- to 6-year-olds) and 2 (6- to 7-year-olds) in Primary School
LDD	Learning Difficulties and Disabilities
LEA	Local Education Authority
OFSTED	Office for Standards in Education
P1, P2	Primary 1, Primary 2: the names given to year groups in Scotland
PS	Partially Sighted
PSHE	Personal, Social and Health Education: a compulsory subject for Primary School pupils to help them integrate with other children and talk about social issues in the wider world
QCA	Qualifications and Curriculum Authority
RCSLT	Royal College of Speech and Language Therapists
SACRE	Standing Advisory Council for Religious Education
SATs	Standard Assessment Tasks (or Tests): the tests and activities given to children at the end of each Key Stage to assess whether they have reached the expected level for a child of their age
SEN	Special Educational Needs
SENCO	Special Educational Needs' Coordinator: the teacher at a Primary School who is responsible for supporting children with learning, behavioural or physical difficulties
VI	Visually impaired

The most current research suggests that as the children move into Key Stage 1 (6-year-olds) there should still be opportunities for them to play alongside more formal learning. Consequently, we should examine the activities which are provided for our under 5s and perhaps consider integrating some of them into our work with the 5 to 7s. Of course this will have big implications in terms of resources and organisation for our children's work.

What is play?

Above all, play is not letting the children loose with boxes of toys and free reign over what they want to do! In fact, this would not only prevent our children learning about God (and be extremely stressful for the people working with them), but most children would also find the lack of structure and organisation deeply unsettling. Children love routine and feel secure when things are well planned and they know what is going to happen in a session. There are many types of play activities which can be built into our sessions with 5 to 7s.

Creative play. This includes play dough, plasticine, clay, junk modelling, cutting, sticking and painting etc. (Play dough is a particularly good activity for anxious children who can play with the dough while observing others as they become used to the group.)

Physical play. Any form of physical exercise is good for children, who, along with the rest of us, lead a more sedentary lifestyle than in the past. Games which involve running, jumping and other forms of movement, as well as dancing, are helpful in using up surplus energy and developing concentration after a time of sitting down and listening.

Musical play. Most children enjoy musical activities. Even if you don't have someone who is able to lead more traditional singing and worship, children love rhythm, clapping games and making sounds with their voices, which can also be accompanied by simple children's percussion instruments, if you are fortunate to have them. These can also be used to help tell Bible stories, with the children having to join in at the appropriate times with the right noises or instruments. Listening to music stimulates imagination, of course.

Role play. This can be linked to the story which is being covered during the session and is explained in more detail in the next section (speaking and listening). 'Small world' toys can also be helpful in this way and are not new by any means (think of the 'Noah's arks' which many Victorian children enjoyed!) Any small Lego or Playmobil figures can be used with additional resources which can be gleaned from charity shops or car boot sales. Some schools have 'Story sacks', each of which contains most of the characters and props to help tell that story. If you are fortunate to have someone who may enjoy creating little bags of resources for particular Bible stories this may be a way to involve other Christians in the work we do with 5 to 7s.

Discovery play. This may include nature walks to enjoy the glories of God's creation, or cooking and eating (for example, making and eating manna). Doing something, as well as talking about it, helps us remember and is much more fun for everyone.

The importance of speaking and listening

At school, speaking and listening is now incorporated into most areas of the curriculum quite aside from its more obvious role in literacy. Many young children, as we have seen, are not yet able to communicate through writing or recording their thoughts and ideas on paper.

Different models of learning

This helps children to develop relationships with those who are working with them.

Shared learning

This is when leaders work with the children to produce something together, relying heavily on the children's input. For example, children and adults may work together to produce a short drama to show in church, telling the story of Moses. The children may decide on the important things they want to include and help to 'write' the script. Leaders and children then act out the drama together.

Guided learning

This is when leaders help a small group of children to produce something of their own. Making a specific type of Christmas card using materials provided by adults would be a good example of this form of working with children.

Modelling

This is merely showing children how we might do something ourselves. We have already seen how children mimic the behaviour of adults and the concept of modelling relies heavily on this. An adult may show children how they would make Noah's ark using junk or construction equipment such as Lego and then allow the children to construct their own.

Guided learning is perhaps the most common method we use currently to work with our young children, but it relies heavily on adult preparation. Whilst carefully thought out preparation is essential in any children's work, guided work does not allow for much spontaneity or children's own input. By combining guided learning with more shared and modelled work we are allowing children to take more ownership of what happens in our sessions and helps us to understand them more and develop our relationships with them. We almost need to plan for more unstructured spur-of-the-moment times, while at the same time being very clear about the focus for each session. This is not as hard as it seems if we allow time for children to talk and play as well as completing the tasks we have prepared. After all, if we do not manage to fill in the sheet for this week but have been able to talk about and meet with God together we have fulfilled our task of enabling children to get to know and love our heavenly father.

Chapter Link

Chapter 7 explores the insights of Godly play.

Speaking and listening is an ideal way to help children learn. Today's children are used to conversing with others verbally about many different things at school in this structured way. We can use some of these activities to help us in working with the 5 to 7s.

Developing our own relationships with 5 to 7s, as well as helping them develop a relationship with God, must involve listening to the children and talking with them about things which are part of their world. Only when children learn to trust those around them will they be able to trust God. All relationships hinge on good communication, much of which is verbal. So we should place enormous importance on developing our own communication skills if we are to be effective workers in helping young children to know and love God.

For example, whilst we may have prepared material for crafts or worksheets for the children to learn about a Bible character one Sunday morning, allowing children to share something which they are excited about, or is making them worried, is of far more importance. If children's feelings and thoughts are brushed away in the need to present the material for that session, then children will not learn anything about that particular story. They will also be left feeling that they and their concerns are not valued and subsequently are unimportant to God. As we saw in chapter 1, Jesus himself famously had time for children in Matthew 19. Jesus was the ultimate 'people person'. He always seemed to have time to listen to others and share with them and we should model ourselves on him.

Circle time

'Circle time' is when children sit in a large group on a carpet and are expected to take turns in sharing their news or expressing their feelings or views. A small toy such as a teddy is used as the 'speaking object' and is passed around the circle and only the child who has the object is allowed to talk, apart from the adult who is facilitating the discussion. This values the contributions made by each child and offers a crucial insight into how children are thinking. This could be adapted and used as an activity when starting our 5 to 7s' sessions. Make three simple 'smiley' faces and place them in the middle of the circle: one showing a happy face, one a sad face and one an 'alright' face. Briefly go round the circle and let the children choose the face which best represents their feelings. Immediately you will gain an insight into each child's life and as time passes and the children develop their relationship with you, their worries and anxieties may surface, which can be used later as a springboard for prayer.

Talk partners

Children are also used to working alongside a 'talk partner' in school, where they discuss something with a friend for a very short time (up to a minute) and then share with the larger group. This enables all children to participate more fully and help them to feel that they are being heard. For example, children could listen to a Bible story and then the group leader could ask them to talk with their partner about some of the issues the story may raise. As well as helping the children to focus on the important aspects of the story and how it may relate to their own lives, it also encourages children to talk about their faith in a natural way with others, which may have repercussions beyond the actual group itself.

Jesus as the ultimate expert in speaking and listening

Read John 4: 3–30 as a group.

One person can read the questions and comments that Jesus made and another person the ones that the woman made.

Notice how far both Jesus and the woman were affected by the situation that they found themselves in.

Notice what sort of questions Jesus and the woman ask.

What questions are:

- Factual ones. (teasing out specific information)
- Closed ones. (requiring a simple answer and no discussion)
- Open ones. (requiring more thought and discussion)
- Experienced ones. (needing a personal, emotional and experiential response)
- Rhetorical ones. (not needing an answer at all)
- Leading ones. (requiring serious thought in a specific direction)

How far do the woman and Jesus answer each other's questions?

What information do Jesus and the woman give each other that then leads on to the next question or comment?

What sort of listening is going on?

Who listens more?

Try to trace the way that Jesus leads the discussion with the woman. How far might you say that Jesus manipulates the conversation – and is that OK because he is in the right position to do so?

What do you think the woman has learnt by the speaking and listening that she and Jesus have been engaged in?

Think over conversations you have had with your group of children recently.

How much have you listened to what a child has said? What may have made it difficult for you to understand them?

How much have they listened to you? How have you helped them to listen?

How much speaking have you done?

How much speaking have they done? How have you helped them to speak?

How much speaking and listening went on between the children themselves?

Drama

The role of drama in speaking and listening can be underestimated. Some children learn best by doing things, and acting out a story will be much more memorable than merely hearing the story. Adults may narrate a story or one of the older children can retell it as the other children pretend to be the various people. For example, it would be much more fun and more memorable to be Joshua and the Israelites walking round the walls of Jericho, than merely hearing the story told or filling in a sheet.

Another related activity is 'hot seating' where someone (it can either be the group leader or one of the children) pretends to be a character from the story and everyone else asks them questions. Additional props, if they are available, always make this more exciting for young children! So, some of those costumes only used for the annual nativity play can be dusted off and put to good use!

When discussing complex and controversial issues which may arise from some Bible stories, it may be useful to play the game 'Conscience Alley'. Here the children make two lines facing each other with a single child who walks between them. Each side takes one point of view. For example, the child about to walk through the 'alley' may be Jonah and each side represents different parts of his conscience, one side telling him to go to Nineveh and the other persuading him to run away. This sort of activity can be really helpful in understanding how different people from the Bible acted and can lead to a discussion about how the children would behave in such a situation.

You might be thinking that this educational approach is far beyond what you can do with your group of 5 to 7s. The truth however is that without knowing it, you are probably already doing much of what is intentionally being done in schools. However the suggestions above should stimulate you to think about how you talk with the children, how you plan a variety of activities for your group, how much play you build into your time together and just what it is reasonable to expect of them. All children's leaders know that they still have much to learn. No one is a perfect children's worker. So, what are you going to be and do differently as a result of reading this chapter?

Chapter 4 – 5 to 7s similarities and differences

While we are all – as human beings – made in the image of God, we are also unique, known to God as separate and special individuals; and the children we work with are equally different, each one precious to him. Just as we need to think about how the physical, social, emotional, intellectual and spiritual development of children affect the way in which we work with young children, we need to consider other differences when planning activities for our 5- to 7-year-olds.

Boys and girls

Perhaps the most obvious difference between children is that of gender. Those of us who are parents will know that, however hard you try to provide a whole range of play materials for our children, toddlers tend to gravitate towards very gender-specific toys. A quick glance into a Nursery or Reception classroom will confirm this. During child-initiated play sessions boys will generally be outside playing on the bikes and large equipment or making things from construction materials such as Lego, while girls are likely to be working in the role play area or making things in the creative area. Despite the best efforts of their teachers it is very difficult to encourage children to go against their natural instinct and play with alternative toys.

There has been a vast amount of research into the reasons for this, linked to the whole debate of the role of nature versus nurture, but the fact remains that, as a general rule, boys and girls are different and they play and learn very differently. Some of the differences between the sexes can be explained by the way the brain is constructed and functions, enabling girls (and women) to perform more than one task at a time while boys generally have greater spatial awareness. Girls also tend to reach the accepted 'developmental milestones' before boys. They are often toilet trained earlier and speak, read and write more fluently at an earlier age than their male peers. However, research suggests that by the age of 8 these discrepancies are less obvious and boys have caught up with the 'expected' levels. This means, however, that the differences between boys and girls of 5 to 7 are quite marked and we need to take account of them when planning our sessions. It may be that if we are working in a large group we consider the whole issue of gender when splitting into smaller groups. Girls often love to work in groups with other girls and boys like to be with other boys. It is not until the teenage years that children become more interested in being with members of the opposite sex.

Boys
- Prefer to play with large equipment such as slides, climbing frames, bikes etc.
- Enjoy playing very physical games like football.
- Like to run around and chase each other in games like 'tag'.

Raising Boys – Stephen Biddulph

At around six years of age, a big change takes place in boys. There seems to be a sudden 'switching on' of boys' masculinity at this age. Even boys who have not watched much TV suddenly want to play with swords, wear Superman capes, fight and wrestle, and make lots of noise. Something else happens that's really important: it's been observed in all societies around the world. At around six years of age, little boys seem to 'lock on' to their dad, stepdad, or whichever male is around and want to be with him, learn from him and copy him. They want to 'study how to be male'. (page 11)

Talk about what implications this need to search for male role models might have for a church community?

- Find it hard to sit still for any length of time.
- Find it difficult to concentrate for long periods of time.
- Tend to give up more easily when they find something difficult.
- Find listening harder at all ages, as they have less sensitive hearing than girls.
- Communicate less orally.
- Have less developed language skills.
- Read fluently at a later age than girls.
- Develop their fine motor skills at a later age, which means that they find accurate colouring or writing harder than girls.

Girls
- Feel less confident when playing on large play equipment such as slides, climbing frames, etc.
- Often prefer playing with outdoor equipment, such as balls or skipping ropes, individually.
- Prefer playing board games to games which need greater spatial awareness, such as football.
- Can sit for longer than boys.
- Have a greater concentration span.
- Are more likely to persevere with something when it is difficult.
- Listen more carefully.
- Talk more with each other.
- Communicate in different ways with different people and have more advanced language skills than boys of the same age.
- Tend to learn to read earlier.
- Enjoy making things which require good fine motor skills and can write at an earlier age. Their writing also tends to be controlled and much neater than boys of a comparable age.

Of course, there are exceptions to every rule and we should be aware that there are children who may not fit into these neat categories! We do need, however, to consider the ratio of girls to boys at any given time as this should influence the activities we provide for them.

There is a lot of debate at the moment about how boys are perceived to be failing within our education system and their achievements are lagging behind those of girls. This is partly due to the fact that traditionally schooling has involved a lot of sitting, listening to an adult and then doing something which requires sitting at a table, concentrating for a considerable period of time and reasonable fine motor skills. If we provide a lot of 'girl friendly' activities such as craft activities and worksheets (which we may have done in the past) for our 5 to 7-year-olds without considering the needs of boys we will quickly begin to alienate them, especially as current research shows they tend to give up more easily than girls. Practically speaking it may be more difficult to offer activities which boys will tend to enjoy, as there is the whole issue of space and resources. However, with some creative thinking we can work around this by doing more physical things such as playing games, singing action songs,

Observing differences between boys and girls

In one of your sessions, arrange to sit as an observer, paying particular attention to how the boys and girls respond differently throughout the session. If you have enough adult helpers, you could have one person observing the girls and one the boys. Watch out for the differences in:

- How they come into the room. What did they do with their coats and belongings? How did they say good-bye to the person who brought them?

- How quickly they settle down. What did they do first?

- How did they listen to the story? How did they participate in any group discussion? Did they sit still or wriggle?

- Did they join in with any singing? Did they join in the praying?

- Given a choice, what did they choose?

- If there were physical activities, how far did the boys and girls differ in the way they joined in?

- What sort of questions did they ask? What insights did they share?

- How did they relate to the others in the group, adults, boys and girls?

- What, if anything, surprised you about the differences?

having simple physical work outs with stretches, running on the spot and jumping, acting out stories, going for walks and so on. Boys will then not only have expended some of their energy and need for physical exercise but all the children will be able to concentrate and sit and listen for longer.

Children with Special Educational Needs (SEN)

According to a recent House of Commons Select Committee on Education and Skills around 1.45 million children were categorised as having some sort of special educational needs (SEN) in England alone in 2005, which is about 18% of all pupils. Most of these children are educated in mainstream schools and it is rare to find children of 5 to 7 years of age in special schools, unless they have a diagnosed disorder or a physical disability of some kind. This is largely because although children may have been identified as having a learning difficulty it takes a long time for children to obtain a statement of SEN.

There is some evidence to suggest that boys are more likely to have SEN than girls. There are, for example, twice as many boys as girls with statements of SEN in general. This rises to five times as many for the fastest growing types of special needs—behavioural, emotional, and social difficulties (BESD), and Autism Spectrum Disorder (ASD). Children from underprivileged backgrounds are also more likely to have SEN, although there is no clear reason why this may be the case.

This means that we can expect at some time or another to have children with SEN in our 5 to 7s' groups. It is more likely that we will be aware if children have SEN within our regular Sunday groups, as we probably have more direct contact with the parents, but when children only come during the school holidays or after school for clubs we may be unaware of any learning or behavioural difficulties they may have. Understanding the general pattern of physical, social, emotional, intellectual and spiritual development of our 5s to 7s (chapter 3) will help us to recognise any specific needs children may have.

It would be impossible (and also inappropriate here) to describe every type of special educational need we may find within our 5s to 7s but there are several which are more common and which we can learn to identify easily. In turn this will help us to understand the children we work with more fully and enable them to feel loved and accepted by both us and God when in many places and situations they may feel unimportant and unwelcome.

1) Dyslexia

Dyslexia is a specific learning difficulty which scientists now believe is neurological in origin. It is more likely to occur in boys than girls and often runs in families. Up to 4% of the population are thought to be affected to a significant extent by dyslexia. As many as a further 6% of the population may be affected to a lesser extent, but some suggest that the percentage may be higher. It is quite difficult to recognise if a young child may be dyslexic, as some children do not learn to read and write until they are 8 but there are several things which may indicate a child is dyslexic to some degree.

Characteristics of children with dyslexia:

- May find it difficult to follow a series of instructions or directions.

- May not be able to hear rhymes and may jumble up words when they say them.

- May reverse numbers, letters or even whole words.

- May spell the same word many different ways.

- May be a reluctant writer.

- May have difficulty tying shoe laces and dressing themselves.

- May have a poor sense of direction and confuse right and left.

- May find it hard to clap a simple rhythm.

- May appear to be clumsy and awkward, tripping over things and be generally unaware of the space around them.

- May find skipping, hopping, throwing and catching difficult.

- May lack confidence and have a poor self-image.

- May surprise you because in other ways they are bright and alert.

The play, speaking and listening activities suggested in chapter 3 will be particularly useful when working with dyslexic children. Play enables all children to find their own level of competence and feel secure as no demands are being made of them in terms of writing or reading. Often dyslexic children are gifted orators and speaking and listening activities will be something at which they can excel and which will build their self-esteem and confidence which is often dented at school or even at home when they are perceived to be falling behind their peers. If we always provide activities which require reading and writing these children may become discouraged, clearly aware that they are unable to do some of the things their peers can complete with ease. This is not to say that we should not read the Bible or do fill-in sheets with puzzles which require writing with our 5s to 7s, but we need to think creatively about how to support these children, if we do. For example, we may be able to pair a dyslexic child with one who finds reading and writing easy as they work with a particular sheet and then allow the dyslexic child to feed back on what they have found out. Not only are young children used to working in pairs in school, they will both have been assigned an aspect of the task and feel equally valued. Alternatively, we may offer a range of activities as follow-up after a Bible story, not all of which will require the ability to read and write.

2) Physical Disabilities

Of course some physical disabilities are immediately apparent. It is not difficult to notice someone in a wheelchair or someone who needs glasses because of impaired vision. However, there are some 'hidden' physical disabilities which some of our 5 to 7s may have, of which the most common are hearing problems and difficulties with speech and language.

a) Hearing loss

Many young children have poor hearing. Of these, very few require a hearing aid or other mechanical devices to improve their hearing. Most hearing problems in the 5 to 7s are caused by a condition known as 'glue ear'. In fact it is estimated that up to 27% of children in this age group will suffer from 'glue ear' at least once in their first few years at school. 'Glue ear' is a condition which tends to affect more boys than girls in which sticky glue-like fluid builds up in the middle part of the ear. It can occur after a cold, as a result of an ear infection or as an allergic reaction to pollen, dust mites, pets, etc. In some children the condition comes and goes, so it is difficult to diagnose, although children who tend to shout may well have a problem with their hearing as opposed to being unable to behave appropriately. Children with persistent 'glue ear' are usually treated by the insertion of grommets which drain the sticky fluid from the ear and improve hearing. However, most children's 'glue ear' is not sufficiently bad to warrant such treatment and so we can expect to have children with some hearing loss in our groups at any given time.

How can we help children who may have hearing loss?
- Understand that some children's frustration or 'bad behaviour' may be due to dulled hearing.
- Cut out background noise while talking to the children. A carpet helps to cut down background echo. Hard church hall floors do not help children with a hearing loss!
- Sit in a place where the light falls clearly on your face, so that your lips can be seen

Useful websites:

British Dyslexia Association **www.bdadyslexia.org.uk/**

Dyslexia Action **www.dyslexia-inst.org.uk/**

Dyspraxia **www.dyspraxiafoundation.org.uk/**

Speech, language and communication difficulties **www.afasic.org.uk/**

ADDISS (ADHD) **www.addiss.co.uk/**

Learning Disability **www.mencap.org.uk/**

MIND (Mental Health Charity which has a lot of useful leaflets about Autism, Asperger's Syndrome, ADHD etc) **www.mind.org.uk/index.htm**

National Autistic Society **www.nas.org.uk/**

Asperger's Syndrome **www.aspergerfoundation.org.uk/**

RNID (hearing impaired) **www.rnid.org.uk/**

RNIB (sight problems)
www.rnib.org.uk/xpedio/groups/public/documents/code/Internet Home.hcsp

Brain Gym **www.braingym.org.uk/**

CURBS (children in urban situations) **www.curbsproject.org.uk**

clearly by the children.

- Sit at the same level as the children, so that you are face to face.
- In certain instances it may be useful to attract an individual's attention by speaking their name before talking to them.
- Speak clearly and possibly more loudly than usual, although there is no need to shout.

These strategies will not only help children with hearing problems but will enable us to communicate better with all the children we work alongside.

b) Speech and language difficulties

In recent years there seems to have been a rise in the number of children who suffer with some form of speech and language problem. OFSTED recently reported that many children in Nursery and Reception classes had poor communication skills with boys again being identified as a concern. A few of these may be due to, or exacerbated by, schools which place a high priority on teaching the three Rs before the children are ready. Even schools which enjoy an environment which is rich in opportunities for play, speaking and listening will be unable to make up for a lack of communication at home. Some nurseries report that children are coming to school at the age of 3 with no language whatsoever, so many 5 to 7-year-olds may consequently be unable to express themselves adequately. This is compounded when a child's mother tongue is not English. As we see increasing numbers of families coming from Africa and Eastern Europe to join the more traditional ethnic minority groups from the Caribbean and the Indian subcontinent, this may be an issue for those of us in churches in multicultural areas.

In its most simple form some children may have a problem with pronouncing certain sounds which can make them difficult to understand. However, a few children may have problems with expressing themselves clearly as they have a language disorder which means they find it hard to put the right words in the correct order. Some children may have a problem with processing or understanding language as well as being able to express themselves.

There are many things we can do to help these children. Obviously the kind of speaking and listening activities which the dyslexic child may enjoy may be traumatic for these children, so we should allow them to participate only in so far as they are able and willing. Forcing children to share something verbally when they struggle with speech will make them feel uncomfortable and unwelcome. For these children play, creative tasks or physical activities will be more enjoyable. Additionally, it cannot be stressed enough that for children with some form of speech and language difficulty we should provide a lot of visual support. For example, when telling Bible stories visual aids like puppets, pictures, and particularly real life objects which are related to the story will be very useful in helping children to understand. These will also help those children who have hearing problems as well as enriching the experience for all the children.

Resources

Top Tips on Welcoming Special Children

Find out what the Bible has to say on helping children with special needs. Be encouraged and inspired with stories from group leaders and parents and equipped with lots of practical ideas.

ISBN 978 1 84427 126 9

£2.99

Top Tips on All-age worship

An inspirational look at why all-age worship is not only desirable but do-able in your church! Explore some of the features of an all-age church and think about the different components of a worship service and how to use them. Plus practical pointers on issues such as planning, leadership and getting creative.

ISBN 978 1 84427 125 2

£2.99

Chapter Link

Chapter 6 looks at various approaches to storytelling.

3) Attention Deficit Hyperactivity Disorder (ADHD) and Attention Deficit Disorder (ADD)

ADHD and ADD are a range of problem behaviours linked to a poor attention span. It is estimated that almost 2% of the UK population may show signs of ADHD and for the most part these are children who are more likely to be boys. Both ADHD and ADD may prevent children from both learning and socialising. However, it is often difficult to identify whether a child has one of these conditions as opposed to something like poor hearing, dyslexia, some degree of Autism, Tourette's syndrome or even minor epilepsy, as many of the symptoms may be very similar. Usually a diagnosis needs to be made by a doctor based on evidence from a range of professionals who have worked alongside the child. This is unlikely to be made until the child has started school as the symptoms may not be so evident at home.

Clearly these are a set of very challenging and difficult behaviours, particularly as many children with ADHD or ADD tend to be very confrontational and defiant, often refusing to comply with the accepted social norms of the group. Some of them may also be deliberately deceitful and destructive and will lie, steal and cheat. However, it is worth remembering that up to 30% of children with one of these conditions may also be suffering from clinical depression and anxiety disorders, so we, as the family of God, need to be especially accepting of these children, particularly as they (and their parents) may feel unwelcome in most social situations.

Whilst in some countries children with ADHD or ADD tend to be given medication (usually Ritalin) to alleviate some of these symptoms (and indeed these may be necessary for some children) there are many strategies we can use to help them to behave more appropriately.

- Have a regular structure to all group sessions, so the child knows what to expect each time. This gives all children a sense of security, but can be especially important for children with ADHD or ADD.
- Be very specific in what you want the child to do. So instead of just asking the child to 'behave properly' we might ask him or her to play with the Lego or look at a book for five minutes.
- Set clear and easily understood boundaries, which are appropriate for the child.
- Be consistent in enforcing these boundaries.
- Refuse to accept inappropriate behaviour.
- Have a system of rewards, such as stickers, to encourage good behaviour which should be used as often as possible to emphasise the positive. Try to 'catch' the child behaving well and emphasise how pleased you are with him or her.
- Use sanctions when the child oversteps the boundaries. If you have been clear in setting these up and explaining them, these will be understood by the child. 'Time out' from the rest of the group may be an appropriate sanction and an egg timer for five minutes could be used to allow the child to calm down.
- Only use sanctions when absolutely necessary. We want children to feel positive about themselves to help them understand how God loves and accepts them as they are and the number of rewards should always exceed the sanctions where possible.
- Communicate with the child on a one-to-one basis if possible.

Characteristics of children with ADHD or ADD:

- Are easily distracted.

- Lack concentration, even when playing, and flit from one thing to another.

- Appear not to listen to others when spoken to.

- Are usually noisy.

- Talk excessively, often without any reference to anything else that others may have said.

- Interrupt verbally or physically, intruding on others' games.

- Blurt out things at inappropriate times.

- Are unable to 'take turns' in games or conversations.

- Will be unable to sit still for any length of time.

- Are likely to fidget and be restless, to the extent that they may simply get up and move around.

- May run around and climb on things.

Of course, there are no easy solutions when working with children who have either of these conditions. If there are other people within the church who can offer individual support for the child as you manage the rest of the group this would be useful, especially if someone is willing to commit to working alongside the child on a regular basis. This would help the child to develop a relationship and the all important sense of security, love and acceptance that he or she needs.

4) Autism

There has been much discussion about autism and its causes lately, with speculation that the MMR vaccine may be responsible for a perceived rise in children who show signs of being autistic to some degree. Though this has not been proved one way or the other, what is certain is that autism remains relatively unknown and misunderstood, despite being identified as a 'condition' since 1943. An estimated half a million families in the UK are affected by autism, which is a lifelong condition that affects everyday social interaction. Often those people on what is termed the 'autistic spectrum' (as there are varying degrees to which individuals are affected by the condition) may have additional learning difficulties as well as being unable to make sense of the world around them.

However, there are a group of autistic people who may find socialising difficult but are average or above average intellectually and usually these are said to have Asperger's syndrome. Often they have poor motor skills. A small number of people with Asperger's syndrome may be exceptionally gifted in a particular way, being able to draw things with huge attention to detail or to calculate with large numbers mentally, such as the character Dustin Hoffman plays in the film *Rainman*.

It is difficult to make any general recommendations about how we can help children with ASD (Autistic Spectrum Disorder) as each child's symptoms will be very unique and require specialised medical intervention or therapeutic treatment. If possible, chatting with the parents may be helpful in knowing the strategies being used with the child.

Although it would not be feasible to suggest carrying out a detailed programme with an autistic child, here are some general principles which may help:
- Demonstrate God's love and acceptance of the child. This goes without saying for all the children we work with, but is particularly important for children on the autistic spectrum, who need to know that they are valued in a world which often makes no sense for them.
- Have patience and understanding. Again this is something we all need when working with our 5s to 7s, but children with ASD may exhibit particularly challenging behaviour.
- Keep sessions very structured, predictable and ordered to provide security for the child. This is, of course, something which will benefit all young children.
- Have a quiet area where the child can retreat to, when things become too much for them. Research suggests that, unlike most children, the autistic child becomes traumatised when their senses are bombarded. Noisy environments in particular can be very unsettling for them as can places where there are a lot of visual stimuli. A quiet place can provide a rest for an autistic child and prevent difficult behaviour.

Characteristics of children with Autistic Spectrum Disorder:

- Are more likely to be boys. The ratio of those with autism is one girl for every four boys.

- Will have difficulty interacting socially with others.

- Will have difficulty communicating both verbally and non-verbally, failing to recognise facial expressions, gestures or tone of voice.

- Will have problems imagining things, such as being able to identify with the feelings of others.

- Will be even more literal than most 5- to 7-year-olds! So 'following' Jesus for them will literally mean walking behind Jesus rather than viewing Jesus as a friend.

- May do some things repetitively for no obvious reason.

- May be very resistant to change.

- Can appear to be uncontrollable and naughty.

- Encourage the child to participate, without coercing them into situations which are likely to be difficult for them. Children on the autistic spectrum will find it hard, for example, to participate in drama and role play activities.
- Use picture symbols or photographs to help them. For some children with autism written words may be easier to understand than verbal instructions (quite the opposite to the dyslexic child). If these are accompanied with simple line drawings this can help them even more.

5) Other children with SEN

Although these are the most common special educational needs there may be other children who stand out from the rest of the children we work with and who may require help. Broadly these fall into two categories: those who are of low general ability, and those who are what is termed in educational circles as 'gifted and talented'. Without going into huge detail these are simply the children who are either not as able as most children or those who are exceptionally able for their age. As a general rule if we offer a wide variety of activities (play, speaking and listening, creative, physical and ones more traditional such as completing worksheets), most children will enjoy what we offer them and not be bored and therefore inclined to make mischief! It may be necessary to provide support for less able children with some activities (perhaps from other adults or as part of a pair with a more able child) and have more intellectually challenging tasks or even additional 'extension' activities to stretch the more able children when they have completed the set task. Some of the things we offer to our 8- to 11-year-olds may be appropriate for these gifted children, but we must not forget that socially and emotionally they are still young children and need to be treated as such.

A mother of a boy with severe learning difficulties, whose story is on the opposite page has written the following:

'Children with disabilities are children. The single most important thing for churches to do is to welcome all children and to become their friends. So the approach for a child with a disability (no matter how severe the disability) is the same as that for any child. Be welcoming. Be warm. Look at the child and talk to them even if they can't talk to you. Welcome their parent or carer. Invite them to join in. Ask the parent to go along with you at least to begin with while you get to know the child, if they have a significant disability. Look for a befriender for that child. This is not an expert who knows everything, but someone (or several people in rotation) who can be especially aware of that child's needs and get to know the family. Don't be scared to ask either the child or their parents what they find helpful and what is unhelpful. Every child is different. No parents will expect experts on hand... they will be hoping for a welcome and friendship.

'Be flexible in deciding which group best suits a 5-7s child with a disability. For some children their own peer group will be best, but for the occasional child it is more appropriate to be with younger children, providing this suits the children generally. If nothing seems to work, don't let families walk round the outside of church in all weathers until the service is over when they can collect their other children! Always offer a cup of tea or juice and search for a place that

A mother of a boy with severe learning difficulties, who has worked hard to ensure her son feels part of a church community has written the following story:

One day, our-father-in-heaven clapped his hands, cleared his throat, and said, 'We're going to have a new arrival on earth.'

The angels stopped what they were doing and looked up.

'A boy,' the father continued, 'called Michael'.

(Murmurs of 'good name' rose from all around.)

'Special,' said the father. 'People will call him disabled'.

With a rustle of wings and padding of feet the angels crowded round the father, faces upturned, alight with love.

'His body will grow, but his mind won't learn very much; he won't be able to play and talk like other children…

'Hey! Careful!' the father cried as angels muscled around him, shining-faced, looking hopeful.

'You know the rules,' he said in joyful mock solemnity. 'Only one angel to one child.'

'Me!'

'No, me!'

'I'd be great.'

Cries came from all around.

(Continued on page 83)

Chapter Link

Chapter 8 explores how all-age worship can be made appropriate for people with special needs.

the child and their parents/carer can sit and if they have to go outside find somewhere suitable for them to sit. Perhaps you could make a bit of the church garden 'sensory' with things to touch and smell and listen to ... to let the child know God loves them. It is helpful to ask all parents to fill in a short form giving information about their child.'

Different learning styles

Developing a nurturing, loving, trusted relationship with the young children we work with is the most important factor in helping them to go on to develop their own relationship with Jesus Christ. However, we are still called upon to teach our 5 to 7s about God and the way in which he has related to his people in the past.

A 'multi-sensory' (using many senses) approach to working with young children is the most effective way we can communicate these truths to our children. It also enables us to meet the needs of all the children we work with, regardless of their age, gender or ability. In many ways this is nothing new and is in itself very biblical. The very act of Communion which Jesus instituted involves using all our senses. It may be no coincidence that the traditional festival of Passover begins with a child asking the question, 'Why do we celebrate this meal tonight?' Research suggests that each of us learns in many different ways using all our senses and the best 'teaching' involves using as many of them as possible, whatever our ability. However, each person – and children are no exception – usually has a preferred learning style.

Visual learners

For about 30% of us visual stimuli help us to understand things. Images and pictures will be our primary helpers. For children who are visual learners looking at the pictures in a book, watching a DVD of a Bible story or watching the images on a PowerPoint presentation will help them learn about God.

Auditory learners

Around another 30% of us prefer to learn in an auditory way. Speaking and listening will be the main things which help these children learn about God, so learning memory verses, role play, puppetry, sharing things verbally in discussions, and praying aloud will be particularly helpful when teaching these children about God.

Kinaesthetic learners

The rest of us – 40% – are kinaesthetic learners. That means we learn by doing things. Hands-on activities such as creative tasks like art or cooking, playing with small world toys, physical activities like singing and dancing, as well as acting out stories, will help kinaesthetic learners learn about God.

When we provide all these kinds of learning experiences in a session a staggering 90% of us will remember what we have learnt in comparison to when we only provide one kind of learning experience. Multi-sensory teaching will meet the needs of all the children we work with, which is vital in a diverse group of 5- to 7-year-olds. Whilst all children will benefit and

(Continued from page 81)

'Wait! Listen,' said our-father-in-heaven.

'Michael will get into lots of scrapes because he will find it hard to learn. He'll fall off cliffs, climb on roofs, run through glass windows, eat all sorts of bad things and his speciality will be jumping into water. You'll have to be fast and strong.'

'I'm your angel,' said one.

'No, me,' said another.

'I'm tough,' said a third.

The angels started flexing their muscles like Mr Universe.

The father held up his hand for silence.

'He won't have many friends, and most people won't talk to him.'

'I want to be his friend.'

'And me.'

'And me.'

'Me ple-e-e-ase!'

'But he will love music,' continued the father.

'Let us through,' called the angel choir, and angels came flocking forward from as far as the eye could see, carrying lyres and harps. One had a drum set.

'Ask us!' they cried.

'… and Michael will know how to worship me,' finished the father.

There was a moment of ecstatic silence, and then, as one, all the angels leapt up, throwing their halos in the air, shouting 'YES!'

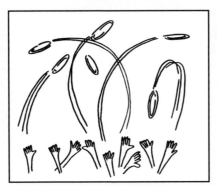

Used with permission of the author, Sally Hodges.

For more information contact:

National Contact Point, 'Through the Roof' PO Box 178, Cobham, Surrey, KT11 1YN

enjoy this learning experience, it is particularly helpful for children with SEN, for whom concentration on one aspect of learning alone may be difficult.

Brain gym

This is a relatively recent innovation in education which may be useful in working with the 5 to 7s. It is a programme which involves using simple movements to integrate the whole brain, the senses and body and has been shown to be effective in improving a wide range of learning, attention and behaviour skills which is obviously particularly useful for children with SEN, but is beneficial to all children. Training is generally recommended and there are a number of resources which are available if you or your church is particularly interested in using it. Page 87 will give you some ideas.

Children with different family backgrounds

Just as each of our children is unique and special, no one family is going to be the same as another. It may be that we run both a Sunday school-based group and an after-school or holiday club and that the families represented at each of these sessions may be quite different. Without generalising and over simplifying, it is more probable that the children who attend groups on Sunday will be from church families whilst those who come along occasionally during the week will probably be from families where these groups provide one more thing to enrich their children's life after school or a means of providing cheap and reliable childcare. It is important that we try to reach out to and understand those children and families who may not otherwise come into contact with Christians.

1) Lone parent families

Social Trends

Perhaps the most obvious exceptions to the traditional and Biblical nuclear family are those with lone parents. Sadly, this is an increasing group of families within our society, even within church circles, as relationships break down and divorce appears to be easier legally, if no less emotionally, socially and often financially painful. Recent statistics suggest a staggering one child in four is being brought up by a single parent, in 90% of cases by the mother. This is more than three times the number of lone-parent families in 1972. Among black ethnic minority groups this is likely to be an even larger figure, with almost half of black Caribbean children being brought up in a lone-parent household. Children from Indian, Pakistani and Bangladeshi communities, however, are less likely to be brought up by one parent, compared with white families.

The absence of a father

In some of these families fathers continue to play a significant part in the child's life, but this is by no means given. Some children have little or no contact with their father at all. According to think tank organisation Civitas, children who grow up without their biological father are more likely to be unemployed, commit crime and leave education early. The implication of this for us as we try to help young children develop a relationship with their heavenly Father is that many of these children may have no conceptual understanding of what a 'father' is at

A session about Noah using a variety of learning styles might include some of the following. Notice the variety in the first word used in each suggestion.

- **Reading** the story of Noah. (visual/auditory)

- **Watching** a DVD of the story. (visual)

- **Acting** out the story. (kinaesthetic/auditory)

- **Talking** about how the characters behaved with a partner or in a group. (auditory)

- **Pretending** to be one of the characters. (auditory)

- **Playing** with 'Noah's ark' or some Lego figures or plastic animals and a shoe box. (kinaesthetic)

- **Singing** songs which may have some relevance to the story. (kinaesthetic)

- **Making** animals from play dough or clay. (kinaesthetic)

- **Making** a dove or raven with paper, painting rainbows, etc. (kinaesthetic)

- **Going** for a walk to look at the world, the creatures and plants God has created. (kinaesthetic/visual)

- **Preparing** something to eat which uses olives or olive oil. (kinaesthetic)

- **Filling** in a word search or crossword, or completing a puzzle or worksheet related to the story. (visual)

- **Learning** a memory verse linked to the story. (auditory)

all, or their idea of a father is very different to the Father we know. While we still need to teach children about God as our Father we need to be very sensitive in how we explain him. It is vitally important that we talk about the different aspects of God, particularly Jesus and the Holy Spirit. These may be far more tangible for some of these children. Even the somewhat 'abstract' nature of the Holy Spirit can be understood by small children, who not only have part of God's spirit within them, but who may even have or have had an 'imaginary' friend.

Economic and emotional implications

Lone-parent families are also more likely to live in rented accommodation or homes which fall below the minimum standards. Michael Scanlan from the Family and Parenting Institute has claimed that these families are more likely to feel the economic and emotional effects of poverty than two-parent homes, as single parents must work longer hours to meet their basic financial needs. As we work alongside these children we have the amazing privilege of not only teaching them about God, but being God's people in a suffering world and offering his love, care and hope for their families.

2) 'Work poor' and 'work rich' families

In addition to the poverty experienced by some lone-parent families, recent research from the Institute for Social and Economic Research indicates that there is an increasing polarisation in our society between families where there are two earners and those where there are none. In March 2007 the Joseph Rowntree Foundation published a report entitled, *Work Rich and Work Poor: three decades of social change*, which describes how, although the total number of people unemployed has decreased overall, there is a significant difference in who is unemployed.

Work poor families

In particular there has been a steep increase in the number of people whose partner also is unemployed. These families are heavily reliant on social security benefits and have very low social incomes, with the accompanying stress and emotional difficulties this may cause and the impact this will almost certainly have on the children. For some children their time spent with us may be a moment of light and order in a world of darkness and chaos, so it is important that we are sensitive to these children's needs.

Work rich families

In contrast over the past 30 years there have been more opportunities for women to work and so some families have benefited financially from having two earners. Higher expectations mean that many families need both parents to work to maintain the standard of living they currently enjoy. However, paradoxically, this may mean that children, whilst materially well off, may be deprived socially of their parents' time and attention. These children may be crying out for someone who will listen to them and understand their world, someone like Jesus, who welcomed children and was interested in them. We are ideally placed to be God's workers in this situation.

3) Cohabitation

In the mid-1960s only 5% of single women lived with a man before they were married. By the

Brain gym

This works on the principle that crossing the mid-line of the body connects the two halves of the brain and helps children become more focused. It also helps if each child has their own bottle of plain water to drink, as research shows this improves concentration further.

Lazy eights

Each child places an arm straight out in front, with their index finger pointing in front at eye level. The child then makes the shape of a number eight lying on its side but can only follow this with their eyes (ie they must not move their head). Repeat with the other hand and arm. (Good for encouraging careful looking.)

Ear lobes

Each child gently rubs the top of their ears and moves down the outside of their ears to the ear lobes. They then gently pull the lobes. (Good for encouraging listening).

Hook ups

Children place their arms straight out in front of them with their fingers hooked together. They then twist their hands so that the palms are turned away from the body and the arms are stretched out. They pull their arms towards their tummy, cross one leg over another and count to ten.

More information about brain gym with accompanying resources can be found at **www.braingym.org.uk/**

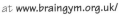

1990s this figure had increased to 70%. Some of those in these relationships view them as an alternative to marriage, but research suggests that less than four percent of cohabitations last for 10 years or more and those with children seem even more fragile and prone to disintegrate. Additionally the fathers in these families are less likely to maintain contact with their children as they do not have the same legal rights as that of a married or divorced father and subsequently less likely to receive financial support. Additionally some parents who have been married may find another partner and move in with them, which brings with it the whole issue of step-families.

All this means that children born to cohabiting parents may be more likely to experience disruption in their lives than those of married couples. As people who work with some of these children we need to be aware of any changes in circumstances which may affect their emotional well-being and be reflected in their behaviour. We must continue to be salt and light to all we meet regardless of their situation. Our example must be Jesus himself who went out of his way to talk to the Samaritan woman at the well in John, chapter 4. You could turn to the exercise in chapter 3 (page 63) where Jesus is the expert speaker and listener. Look at how he accepted this woman and how he showed this acceptance.

Children from different faith backgrounds

Ethnicity

We are increasingly becoming more of a diverse society. Whilst the 2001 census showed that over 90% of people classed themselves as being white, there are significant groups of people from different ethnic minorities within the UK, in particular from the Indian subcontinent (India, Pakistan and Bangladesh), the Caribbean and Africa. As political, economic and social change continues we can expect our society to become even more multicultural. Recent trends show increasing numbers of children from black Africa, and economic workers from Eastern Europe. Certain areas in particular attract high levels of immigration, perhaps because there are already established communities. There is also a growing number of asylum seekers who fall into this category. It is important for us to begin to know and understand these communities as we try to reach out to them and welcome their children into our clubs and Sunday schools.

Faith

Whilst nearly seven out of ten people in the 2001 census classified themselves as white Christian, it is clear that most of these people do not actively participate in church itself. However, the fact that almost 36 million people are happy to identify themselves in this way means that they are happy for their children to come to our after-school and holiday clubs (especially if it helps with the provision of childcare) and learn about the Christian faith, which is a real encouragement to those of us working with young children. It shows what a huge potential there is waiting for us if we are willing to reach out into our local communities.

Most black Caribbean and African people (71%) also profess to be Christians as well as a large number of families of mixed races (52%). Some of these children's experience of

Believing that all children are created in God's image, CURBS starts in the world of the urban child and, through positive relationships, seeks to build bridges which will enable them to experience God's loving care.

CURBS has two main aims:

- To provide Christian resources specifically geared to the needs of inner city children and those on outer urban estates.
- To provide support, training and encouragement for children's workers in such areas by means of networking, training and resource days and partnerships.

For more details visit **www.curbsproject.org.uk**

Christianity (worship, attitudes to children, preaching) will be very different from our own and again we need to be willing to understand and work with these different traditions.

Among other faiths the next largest group is Muslims, who account for almost 3% of the population, followed by Hindus (1%) Sikhs (0.6%) and Jews (0.5%). Many Muslims and Hindus are happy for their children to attend holiday and after-school clubs run by Christians. Indeed a number of Muslims would rather their children attend a school that is run by a Christian denomination than another less overtly faith-oriented school, generally because of the moral values which are promoted at Christian schools. They see Jesus as a very important and unique prophet and consider Christians to be 'people of the book', with whom they have more in common than with the general population. Whist there are obviously fundamental differences in the way we see Jesus compared with the way Muslims view him, in some ways it is often easier to have a conversation about God or Jesus with a Muslim than it is with someone who professes no faith whatsoever. As tensions between Muslims and the rest of Britain have become more evident in recent years, it is vitally important that we build bridges with the Muslim community, so that they and their children learn to trust us.

In all cases, while we should be aware of the backgrounds of the children and families we work with, we should never make assumptions or judgements about them but be sensitive to their needs. For some families this may be their only contact with Christians and we need to be distinctly different from all the other groups they encounter, accepting and loving them in the same way Jesus would have accepted them. For more details read *Top Tips on Welcoming children of other faiths* (SU 2007).

Jo (6) and Anna (4) were going to see Granny and Grandad. Joel said, 'Let's try and be as good as new.'

Jo (5) said, 'I think that great Grandpa is probably mowing God's lawn.'

Jo (5)said, 'Great Grandpa is probably just getting ready for bed in heaven isn't he?'

Jo (5)said, 'Do you know what my favourite part of a children's party is ? I like that there are lots of children and not many grown-ups, so the children have a chance to chat to each other!'

Billy (7)said, 'Love is what's in the room with you at Christmas, if you stop opening presents and listen.'

Hannah said, 'When I grow up I want to be a Christian.'

Tim replied, 'When I grow up I want to be a giraffe.'

A newly qualified teacher was in charge of her first class – year two. The school was a very multi-cultural community and most of the children came from a non-Christian faith background. When the opportunity arose she asked one of the girls if all of the class were Sikhs. The girl was very quick to reply, 'Some of us are six and some of us are seven!'

Chapter 5 – Principles into practice

As you consider working with 5 to 7s, you may find yourself asking a stream of questions such as: 'Why do it at all? Where do we start? What activities are suitable? What sort of programmes shall we put on? Where will we run the activities? When is the best time?' Sit down with a cup of tea or coffee and think through what you are actually trying to do and why. How are you praying about the 5 to 7s and praying about what you are aiming to do with and for them? You will probably find that your thinking and planning is much more constructive if you think and plan with others who share your concern for this age group. Dream dreams, share your hopes and fears and, above all, be honest with each other. Together fill in the checklist on the opposite page as you gather your reflections and ideas.

Why work with 5 to 7s?

There is a strong Biblical base for working with children of all ages and that includes this age group. Take this as your mandate and always keep it in the forefront of your mind as you develop your thinking in all the other areas.

Between the ages of 5 and 7 a child develops rapidly in so many areas. We would be foolish if we omitted spiritual development as part of this overall package. Spiritual development is vital. It is primarily the responsibility of the parent but many parents are happy to pass on at least some of this responsibility to those in the wider church. You might like to reflect on how far parents in your church view you as a partner in spiritually nurturing their children. Do parents leave it all up to the church or think it is all their responsibility? How comfortable are you with the expectations of parents and the church? As children's workers we would want to play our part in this vital role.

Children are an integral part of the church family. It would be to the detriment of our fellowships if there were a 5 to 7s gap in our church community. They may be noisy, active, curious and chaotic, but we would desperately miss them if they were not there. How dull life would be! How lacking in enthusiasm and natural exuberance! What is more, strategically 5 to 7s could be said to be the foundational layer for future children's and youth work in the church. A thriving group for this age will help to ensure that there is a strong 8 to 11s programme leading to a more effective 11 plus programme. All this means that the church has to have a long view into the future. A decade later the 5-year-olds will be at the heart of the youth group. Concepts absorbed at 6 may have to wait ten years to bear fruit and make sense!

As someone reading about working with 5 to 7s, you are either already working with them and want to develop what you do, or you may be at the start of something new. Maybe you are a parent wanting to do the best for your own child or wanting to seize opportunities to work in a church context with the friends of your child. Maybe you have contact with some 4- to 5-year-olds who will soon move into this target age group or you are aware of the potential

Checklist: what we want for our 5 to 7s

What do you most like about 5 to 7s?

What do you least like about them?

What three words would most describe life for a 5- to 7-year-old?

1

2

3

What have you seen that works effectively with 5 to 7s?

What have you seen done for 5 to 7s that is not effective?

What do you think is the most challenging aspect of working with 5 to 7s?

Why do you want to work with 5 to 7s and not another age group?

What might prevent you from more effective work with 5 to 7s?

Remember, there are no standard answers as every situation is different. You will need to bear in mind your local circumstances and work out what is best for you. This may mean a certain amount of trial and error. Don't be worried if something that you have seen working well somewhere else doesn't work for you. Be brave; try a variety of approaches until you find what works best in your situation. See *Top Tips on Encouraging faith to grow.*

opportunities with 5 to 7s. You can never be the perfect 5 to 7s children's worker (such does not exist) but you do want to be as effective as you can, for God's sake and for the sake of the children. 5 to 7s can be great fun. Don't be surprised if you get more out of it than you put in.

What are the possibilities?

Midweek clubs

A midweek club is a chance for children to get together to have some fun, as it says, midweek! Adult helpers get to know the children, teach them, learn from them and enjoy being together. Such clubs meet in a school, at church or in some other building in the community. It will probably last between an hour and an hour and a half. Think carefully about the right time. Is straight after school a good time for this age group? Do you need to provide a drink and a small snack? Is 5–6pm better? The programme should contain a variety of elements but, in a Christian context, would include an element of exploring a Bible story and encouraging engagement with God.

A lunchtime club in a school provides similar opportunities but time is more limited, of course, and is rightly affected by the requirements of the school and the school day.

Advantages:
- You are not under the same restraints of a Sunday which may mean lack of space, needing to be quiet so as not to disturb the adults, not preventing adults from participating in Sunday worship.
- You have more control over the timings and the facilities that are available.
- You can create a relaxed atmosphere.
- You will probably be able to contact a wider group of children than normally attend on a Sunday.
- You may appeal to parents who may be suspicious of something that is overtly 'church'.

Disadvantages:
- It is sometimes difficult to find helpers who are available in the afternoon, just after work or around evening meal time.
- It can be difficult to make a link between the midweek club and the main body of the church.

Midweek community clubs for 5 to 7s already exist such as Beavers and Rainbows, ballet and sports clubs. These will probably increase with the introduction of extended services on school premises. Midweek clubs become much more popular from the age of 8, so there are still opportunities to start early and beat the rush! Most parents are happy for their children to go to a midweek club if they can see that it is well organised and that the leaders are caring, trained and have been appropriately checked.

Getting started brainstorm

In a group, use the following questions to think how you might get started or develop your ministry to 5 to 7s.

- What are the needs of your community and the children in that community?
- What is the target group you are trying to reach? Is it church children, or those who don't come to church, or those in the local school, or a mix of all of these?
- When are the children in your area around and therefore available?
- How is Sunday spent in your community? Are children visiting relatives (especially if the parents are separated)? Are there lots of other attractions or clubs such as football, dance lessons, pony club? Is it a family day or a DIY day?
- Think about the advantages and disadvantages of meeting midweek or on a Saturday? Remember that children go to school (most of the time), get tired easily and bedtime for some 5 to 7s can be quite early. At what time do working parents get home? When do families in your community eat? Do they eat together? Do the children eat early or wait till the whole family is home? Can children get to your venue easily or do they need a lift?
- Consider what seasonal events occur in your locality such as camps, holidays or festivals.
- Are you going to structure your group around academic years? Is it going to operate by key stages as they are in school? Or do you plan to stick to 5 to 7s? There are advantages and disadvantages in each structure. Ultimately, think through what will work best in your situation.
- So what are the options?

Discuss these with the other interested people you have identified. Several heads are better than one!

Holiday clubs

Holiday clubs are what they say they are – clubs for children during school holidays. The main idea is to provide an activity for children during the holiday that is fun, lively and introduces children to Jesus. Many churches run holiday clubs for 5 to 11s. There is nothing wrong with this but it is a very wide age range and it is often the younger ones who are forgotten or get left behind. A 5-year-old is very different from and has different needs to an 11-year-old about to go to secondary school. If you haven't run a holiday club before, why not start small (in more ways than one) with the 5 to 7s. You can expand the age group next year to 5 to 8s.

When is the best 'holiday' period for a club? Traditionally people have opted for the summer holidays. This is a good long time but some children are likely to be away from home at some stage during the summer holidays. Also it can be difficult to follow up the holiday club by the regular children's work, especially if Sunday groups close down during the summer period and the club is early in the holiday period. Some churches run a holiday club during one of the half term breaks in February, May or October. More children may be around then. The weather may be worse so parents could be looking for an indoor activity for their children. Other churches have run a holiday club the same day each week for a specific period, for example, every Monday during the summer holidays or every evening during June.

Advantages:
- They are very effective in building bridges into the local community.
- They provide goodwill and open up new opportunities.
- They allow time to get to know children and build up good relationships with them.
- They provide a good opportunity for learning about God together.
- They are fun.
- They help to reach out to the church fringes.
- They provide training opportunities for church members of all ages and a chance for the Christians in one church or from several churches to serve God together.

Disadvantages:
- They are labour intensive.
- To be fully effective they need to be part of an ongoing work.

Sunday Activities

A Sunday activity can be anything from Sunday School, to Junior Church, to Young Church or even a midweek club style that meets on a Sunday afternoon or early evening. Here we are talking about an activity that takes place while the adults are worshipping at the same time but in a different building or part of the building. Most churches' work for this age takes place on a Sunday morning while the morning service is happening and therefore most (or all) of the children that come are from church families.

Advantages:
- You know the children who will be coming to your group and you can tailor materials and the programme to their needs.

SU resources for midweek eyelevel or holiday club

Holiday club

Champion's Challenge
978 1 84427 270 9

Pyramid Rock
978 1 84427 139 9

Wastewatchers
978 1 84427 204 4

Midweek eyelevel

High Five
978 1 84427 251 8

Target Challenge
978 1 84427 314 0

Rocky Road
978 1 84427 183 2

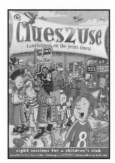

Awesome
978 1 84427 153 5

Streetwise
978 1 85999 767 3

Clues2Use
978 1 84427 113 9

All at £9.99!

- You know the families of the children which helps in your relational work.

Disadvantages:
- It can be difficult to get people to run groups regularly on a Sunday morning.
- The time you have with the children can differ widely depending on how long the preacher takes. The time you have depends on how long the adults need or want.
- The children's work can be seen as less important with adult activities taking priority over venues and resources.
- You rarely have children from outside the church family.

If you are struggling to find helpers, invite anyone who may be interested to visit your programme, as an observer. Let them know that they are not making any long lasting commitment but just looking at what happens.

We would encourage you to move away from the 'Sunday School' image. Some children love school and given the choice would like to spend every minute of every day there; others view things quite differently. On a Sunday the children are not coming to school but they gather to worship, praise, pray and learn. It should be a totally different experience from school. So avoid words such as class, teacher, school, worksheet or lesson and replace with words such as group, leader, club, activity sheet or magazine, and session or group time. Think of an age-relevant, yet snappy, title for your group. The children may have some good ideas, or at least give you some suggestions that can act as a springboard for further discussions.

A good test of how well your group is going is to ask: 'Is this group one worth joining?' If I were a 5-, 6- or 7-year-old would I want to invite my friends along to this group? The answers could be quite revealing.

On page 105 is a collection of titles for a children's club.

Activity clubs

These clubs take a particular subject or hobby and base the club around it. They are mainly used with older children or young people but may from time to time be appropriate with this age group. For example, many football clubs (not the professional ones) start their teams at the age of 7 and this can often be something that draws children (usually at the age of 10 or 11) away from church activities. So why not hire a local AstroTurf area or gymnasium for your 7-year-olds to play football together? I know a local church that runs a football club every Friday evening in a local sports hall. The children of the church attend and invite their friends. It starts with a junior group (coached by adults and some of the older boys) and then the senior boys carry on. There is a two-minute devotional spot between the two sessions. Or is there a Saturday league that they could play in? There may be more opportunities for this with the advent of the extended services provision. Two young men attached to a premier division football club offered to run a football club for the Year 2s at a local infants' school. The head teacher advised them and ensured they had been CRB checked. It was so popular that opportunities were given for Year 1 children to join in, too. Church groups may consider

Splash!

Are you looking for great ideas to make the Bible come alive to 5 to 8s so that it makes a difference in their lives? Each session in *Splash!* unpacks a passage from the Bible in an age-appropriate way for 5 to 8s and gives you ten or more activities to choose from. Each Bible passage is part of a syllabus which ensures children explore the whole story of the Bible, including the well-known and the less familiar stories. To get the best out of *Splash!* you need a *Splash!* leaders' guide for each leader in your group and one Splash! activity magazine for each child.

For more details see **www.scriptureunion.org.uk/light**

Chapter Link

Chapter 8 looks at all-age services and opportunities.

doing the same.

It does not have to be football, of course, but is there some other area of interest among your children like dance, mini-tennis, cookery or art that could act as a focus for a club?

Advantages:
- A chance to build up good relationships with children in a relaxed atmosphere.
- The possibility for those outside the church to join in, if they share the same interest.

Disadvantages:
- It is potentially more difficult to tie activities like this into the main body of the church.
- You will need people who are qualified (or at least have a good understanding) in a particular area such as football coaching and will need to check on CRB and insurance.

Special events

These are one-off activities, often linked to the church calendar or seasons. They are ideal ways of following up a holiday club. For ideas for Christmas, Easter, Pentecost, Harvest, Halloween and Mother's Day turn to pages 152 in chapter 8.

Advantages:
- You can build your programme to suit the needs of the children, the helpers you have and the facilities that are available.
- You can plan them well ahead – to ensure a balanced programme throughout the year.
- It is easier to encourage people to help as they are not committed every week but just certain dates throughout the year.
- Children and parents from a non-church background may find it easier to identify with a seasonal event.

Disadvantages:
- It is hard to build up good relationships with children when you only see them spasmodically.
- The teaching that you do is limited to the church calendar eg Christmas, Easter, Harvest.
- Events that happen at busy key seasonal moments will also be busy times for potential helpers.

Family events

We must never forget that children are part of a family. Families come in all shapes and sizes. There may be times when we want to direct our focus to the child in the family context. How about a special lunch or breakfast at church where the children could serve their mums or dads on Mothers' or Fathers' Day? Is it possible to structure a craft morning for the whole family? For more ideas of families' ministry, get hold of a copy of *Top Tips on Growing faith with families* (SU) by Pauline Burdett.

Suggested annual programme of events for 5 to 7s

January	Post Christmas/New Year party – time to have fun together
February	A Pancake party
	A daytime or early evening event at half-term – most children are around
	Valentine's party
March	Mother's Day
April	Palm Sunday
	Easter – Good Friday, Easter Saturday/Sunday or Bank Holiday Monday
	Holiday club or event in the holidays
May	An outing, trip or picnic or a half-term event
June	Father's Day
July	'Moving on up' session for those moving from KS1 to KS2
August	Holiday club
September	'Let's get going' – to mark the beginning of a new school year.
	Harvest
October	A Light party – alternative Halloween
November	Bonfire night
	Remembrance Day - an appropriate and sensitive session
December	Pre-Christmas session or sessions. This could be held on a Saturday morning to help parents with their Christmas shopping.
	Crib service

Extras

A half day of craft, cooking or sporting event

Trip to a theme park or zoo

A praise and/or thanksgiving session

A creative prayer session

A children's garden party

Some form of nativity play

A short drama or mime

Advantages:
- It is good for the family to be able to do something together rather than being constantly divided up into separate age groups.
- You get to see the children in the context of their families and how they relate to each other.

Disadvantages:
- It can be difficult to plan a programme or activity that covers the whole range of age groups.

Groups that are linked to an external organisation

Some churches have traditionally had a relationship with an external group in order to operate their children's work. For example, Scouts (Beavers aged 6 to 8) and Guides (Rainbows aged 5 to 7).

Denominational groups
- CPAS. Initi8 is the under 8s ministry, providing support and training. For more details contact www.cpas.org.uk.
- The Methodist church. Methodist Children provides regular invaluable e-news and resources. For more details visit www.methodistchildren.org.uk
- Salvation Army. Watch out for news of the children's pages on the main website! www.salvationarmy.org.uk
- Other useful websites are: www.cofe.anglican.org/info/education/children, www.cwanetwork.org.uk, www.baptist.org.uk/resources/children_youth.html

Other wider groupings

Urban Saints

Formally known as Crusaders, Urban Saints runs weekly clubs, special events, holidays, community projects and training programmes for children and young people. They also provide training and resource volunteers to work with 5- to 18-year-olds. Around 20% of their work is with 5 to 7s. Their web address is www.urbansaints.org.

Kidz Klub

Kidz Klub was started in the UK by Nic and Jenny Harding of Frontline Church in Liverpool after being inspired by a similar programme run by Metro Ministries in New York. Children meet on a Saturday morning for an upfront presentation that usually lasts about 1½ hours. It is aimed largely at children with little or no contact with a church community. The main activity is followed up by personal visits to each child and their family in their home later in the week. It requires significant commitment and organisation and has been very effective.
For more details visit www.kidzklub.biz/kidzklub/index.html

Girls' Brigade and Boys' Brigade

Some churches call upon outreach and evangelism movements such as Girls' Brigade (GB)

Tried and tested opportunities

There are many creative ways of working with this age group, as children's workers seek to reach out to those who are outside or on the fringes or to disciple children's faith. Most initiatives with children tend to be with the over 8s but here are two suggestions that have been tried.

Boys' or girls' breakfast. One church has regularly run a men's prayer breakfast on a Saturday morning. They then decided to run a boys' prayer breakfast at the same time. The prayer time needs to be organised in a different way but the boys realise the importance of prayer and how important their role is! They spend quality time together and build up friendships as well as seeing good male role models from the men present. A similar pattern could be adopted for women and girls!

Some churches work to a cell model whereby the congregation is broken down into cells of 8 to 12 people. The idea is that each cell aims to grow to about 16 in number and then divide. Some churches use this model for their children's work as well. So there is a cell group for 5 to 7s numbering about 12 in total. They meet regularly on a Sunday and plan to meet occasionally during the week, with the possibility of a Saturday get together from time to time. They hope and plan that the group will grow to about 16 then they will divide it and create two groups. But churches without such an intentional commitment to cell groups run small discipleship groups for children, although most of these would be for older children. But the concept can be easily adapted to run such a group for younger children too.

and Boys' Brigade (BB) who specialise in providing leadership training, resources and activities for children's work. GB and BB enable churches to build and develop ongoing, focused evangelism among children and young people, many of whom are from non-church backgrounds. The GB's group for 4-rising 8s is called Explorers, and the BB's Anchor Boys group is for 6 to 8s.

Advantages:
- They provide a mission opportunity amongst children on the fringe or otherwise 'outside' church.
- Meeting midweek, the result is a new 'church congregation' that meets to explore and grow in faith.
- The children and leaders gain a sense of belonging and access to a wider group.
- There may be activities organised with a number of other groups.
- Resources and a framework for running ministry with 5 to 8s provides holism and the means to keep going.

Disadvantages:
- There may be a financial cost of 'membership'.
- Historic connections to a particular group may make change and flexibility a challenge.
- Integration into Sunday church is not always the 'right next step' for these children.
- Your church members or leadership team may struggle to see these groups as evangelism and mission, as attendance at Sunday church may not be regular.
- Leadership and succession planning for these groups is a whole church issue, but can often be neglected.

Practicalities

Where will we run the activities?
Many rural and some urban churches struggle to provide adequate space. They have an old church building with fixed pews and no church hall. Creativity is called for. If we are serious about children's work we need to consider the following questions. Is it possible for the church to engage in furniture removals? Is there a school nearby which could be used? Would someone be willing to let you use a room in their house?

When choosing your location, bear in mind that it needs to meet health and safety requirements. Is it warm, clean, adequately lit and well ventilated? The minimum unencumbered floor space for this age group is 25ft^2 (2.3m^2) per child. Does your venue meet this requirement? To find out more detailed information see Full Day care: Guidance to the National Standards under www.ofsted.gov.uk/publications/287

Meeting in Church
Advantages include: children can become familiar with church surroundings. This can lead to curious questions about crosses, stained glass windows and baptisteries!
Disadvantages include: it may be cold; fixed furniture is not flexible; some people are unsure about children being allowed to be noisy and messy in a church building.

The name of your group

The name of your group is one important way of helping the children feel they belong. This name also states who and what you are. Here is a random selection from over 100 church websites of the names used for children's Sunday and midweek groups (not just 5 to 7s). Sadly, many of the group's names had adult, old-fashioned or dull titles. 'Junior church', 'Young church', 'Juniors' or 'Primary' is not the most original, God-inspiring or non-school name! This list may give you some ideas or determination to call your group something that is child-appealing!

Sunshine	Kidstuff	Pebbles
C Club	Kidz Zone	Followers
Sparklers	All Stars	Topz
King's Zone	Pulse	Kids Zone
Splash	The Way	King's Club
Whizz Kids	On Safari	Flames
Rockers	The Roosters	Kids Club (Klub)
Laser	Stepping Stones	J Team
Jam	Stars	Rockets
Take Off	Jammers	Climbers
Fun Club	Promiseland	The Best Club Ever

S.M.A.S.H. (Sunday Mornings Are Special Here)

Fandabidozzie Fridays

Day of the week club eg Wednesday Club, Saturday Special

Chapter Link

Chapter 6 considers some of the building blocks that shape a programme

Meeting in School

Advantages include: schools are designed with children in mind with high standard loos and security; there is usually plenty of space; for those who have reservations about coming into a church building, this can be a good half way house; children are familiar with the surroundings.

Disadvantages include: there are probably financial implications; the school may not have natural links with the church; for the children, it remains school rather than church; children who go to the school will be on familiar territory, unlike children from other schools.

Meeting in someone's house

Advantages include: it ought to be warmer and more personal; it is good for developing relationships with children and parents; in some rural situations it may be the only option.

Disadvantages include: people may not naturally link the home to the church, (which may be an advantage); parents may have some concerns about child protection issues; there are probably limits to space.

Meeting in the village or church hall

Advantages include: it provides more space; it is neutral ground; it acknowledges the place of the local community.

Disadvantages include: not all village or church halls are suitable for children's work; as they are used for a variety of activities they may be dirty or uncared for.

The most important thing about where you meet is that it is a place that children can feel is theirs for the length of the club. Can they put their pictures on the wall? Do other people move their things around? Children need a space or place they can call their own. That is why their place in the classroom at school or their bedroom at home is so important to them. What can you do to ensure that this happens in your activities? If you are working in an area that is used for a multitude of activities you may have to invest in some movable display boards and furniture that enable the children to see the area as theirs. If you have the privilege of working in the same area every time and you can keep your displays up, always remember to take old things down and put new material up. A display that has been up for six months or more can look really sad and messy.

When is the best time?

The best time must be the time that best suits the children and their families. This will differ from situation to situation and you may have to go through a process of trial and error to come up with the right answer. If you decide to run a midweek activity, before you make your final decision, do some research as to what day and which time after-school activities take place. These may take place in school or elsewhere in the community such as gym clubs, ballet lessons, football practice and so on. You want your activity to stand alone. As far as is possible, your activities should not conflict with competing options.

Amit
Aged 6

Cheyenne
Aged 6

Chapter 6 – People and programmes

People

People are the most precious resource that you have. As children grow up they will forget much of the content of what their Sunday group leaders taught or shared with them but they are likely to remember the leaders who did the teaching and sharing. If you think back to your school (or Sunday school) days you will probably remember your teachers or leaders. Can you still picture them? What a responsibility that places on us!

When thinking about who is best for working with children, we normally start by thinking about the knowledge, attitudes and skills that are needed in helpers to make the children's work effective. But before we get to that stage, two vital factors are needed.

A love for God

This must be the primary characteristic we look for in our leaders. If children will remember their leaders more than what they are actually taught, then it is essential that the leaders are as Christ to them. If a person's heart is right with God then many of the skills and much of the knowledge that is needed to work with this age group can be learnt or acquired at a later stage (if they are not there in the first place). This means that their lifestyle demonstrates a Christlikeness. This is not to suggest that you insist that every children's worker is perfect – you will never succeed – but you do need to consider the way that they conduct their relationships, the way they speak, the respect they show, the attitudes they communicate. What would Jesus do?

A love for children

This follows on naturally from the above. A love for God prompts a love for children. This is not something to be taught from a text book or that you can go on a training course to learn, although an effective children's worker can inspire others to follow suit. For some there may be an innate affinity with 5 to 7s. For others this affinity comes with experience and time. For any potential worker with 5 to 7s, there has to come a time when they take that step of faith and get involved in the world of a 5- to-7-year old.

If you are looking for leaders, the first thing to consider is, do they love God and want to serve him? Secondly, do they love children and enjoy being with them?

Sara says: 'I chose to train to teach 5 to 7s because I thought these were the most foundational years in a child's life when I could have the most impact. I also happened to like the age group.'

Colin says: 'I love to work with 5 to 7s because they are so accepting of me as an individual and to the message of Christ that I share. They do not take everything I say at face value but have the ability to question everything. I need to be on my toes to respond to them.'

Job Description for a 5 to 7s children's worker

Hours of work

As long and as often as is needed. This includes preparation time before a session, planning time with the team, the time of the session and prayer time.

Rewards

Knowing the joy of serving God.

Building relationships with children aged 5–7 and other leaders.

Development of ministry gifts.

No financial or status remuneration.

Essential skills and experience

A love for God. (even if you've only been a Christian for a short time!)

Willingness to learn.

Willingness to be part of a team.

Sense of fun.

Patience and caring.

Introvert or extrovert personality.

Male or female.

Over 18 (but younger helpers welcome).

Preferred skills and experience

Love of children aged 5 to 7s and appreciation of their world.

Knowledge and love of the Bible.

Welcomed skills and experience

Ability to sing, play a musical instrument and enjoy music.

Ability to use craft creatively to help children explore truths about God.

Ability to speak and listen with children.

Ability to tell, read and enjoy stories.

Ability to empathise with children.

Ability to use puppets.

Training

However gifted the people on your team of helpers are you will want to instigate some form of in-service or on the job training. Put a new team member with a more experienced leader, especially if the more experienced person has a particular skill that you would want to replicate. For example, if you have a young person joining the team who has some skills in music, why not pair them with the person who normally does your music and singing and let them share in and learn from their expertise?

The second form of training is in the form of an official training session or course. You can either choose to go on a nationally organised course or arrange one for your own church or a group of churches in your community. The advantage of arranging one yourself is that you can choose what to put into the programme and make it more specific to your needs. However, that is more time-consuming and may not be as well constructed as a course that is more widely available. Scripture Union offers both a national training course and has staff who are happy to help organise localised training.

Child protection

Child protection has to concern every church. In 1993, the Home Office issued a document called *Safe from Harm* which provided voluntary organisations with guidelines for safeguarding children and young people in their care. Most mainstream denominations have either taken this document as it stands or slightly adapted it and made it compulsory for all member churches to sign up to it. There may be some churches that are not aligned to one of the mainstream denominations that have not yet adopted this. If you are working with children and young people you must have a policy regarding child protection, and if you haven't, you should correct this immediately.

A church's Child Protection policy should cover a number of key areas, including the following:

- Those who work directly with children. It is not enough for a church to say that everyone has known an individual for years and so they must be suitable to work with children. UK law says they must be checked through the Criminal Records Bureau (CRB) and as a result, have an Enhanced Disclosure – documentation that proves they have no current or spent criminal record that would disqualify them from being in a position of trust with children or vulnerable adults. Make sure that people work to specific guidelines when working with children or talking one-to-one, so that they are never at risk of being accused of any improper conduct.
- Those who work in the vicinity of children will need to be checked similarly. One UK criminal case that has shaped legislation on this issue involved a school caretaker. So, for example, if you run a midweek club at church and the church caretaker is regularly there during this time, or the minister is in his office whilst the club takes place, they will need to be checked through the CRB as described above.
- There should be clear and specific guidelines for those who work with children, to know how to deal with a child who tells them that they are being abused, or whose behaviour,

language or appearance gives rise to suspicion of abuse. Every church should have a designated Child Protection Officer to whom any suspicion or disclosure of abuse must be reported confidentially, and who should then take it on to a higher authority, such as Social Services or the police. The guidelines should also outline what action will be taken in the event of any disclosure, and how those involved should handle any information. Thinking it is for the good of the situation, people in churches are notorious at spreading information to others 'for prayer' but child abuse of any form, whether suspected or known, needs to be handled with extreme care and privacy. Even if the person suspected of abuse is a member of the congregation, a church cannot make their own decisions about how it will proceed; only those recognised under law as being in authority – that is, the police or Social Services – can decide what must be done. Be sure to train volunteers regularly in how to deal with a disclosure of abuse, or any suspicions about it.

Whether or not your denomination has a Child Protection Policy you will find great help from the Churches Child Protection Advisory Services (CCPAS) (see page 160 for website details). They can advise you about creating a policy if you do not have one, and they sell useful resources on this topic, such as small cards that can be kept in a pocket or wallet which outline the action to be taken if abuse is suspected or disclosed.

As well as the legal requirements covered by policies, do consider simple things that can do much to protect children: checking that children leave with the right adult, removing name badges before they leave the building, not leaving documentation lying around so that anyone could see names and addresses. Perhaps the most important ways to keep children safe are to train your team regularly, to encourage best practice in talking with children (ensuring that one-to-one conversations are held within sight, if not sound, of other leaders), and to get to know and understand the children's families.

OFSTED and the Children Act

The Children Act of 1989 lays down certain requirements for working with children. Most of these will not apply to your work with 5 to 7s but you will still need to consider carefully how it may impact your programme. You only have to register with OFSTED (it was originally Social Services) if you are working with a group of children under the age of 8, for more than two hours, on more than six days in any one year. That will probably mean that this legislation will not affect you, but it does lay down various policies considered to be good practice. Here are two that are worth considering:

- When working with 5 to 7s the recognised ratio is one adult to every eight children.
- When running a holiday club you do not need to register with OFSTED but it is considered good practice to inform them of your activities.

In addition, try to establish a team with both genders. Unfortunately, in most churches (and schools) those working with this age group are predominately female. But it is important that children see good male role models as well. Where are the male role models for your children in this age group?

Also make sure your leaders are unshockable. Children this age are not necessarily innocents, full of sweetness and light. They also have the ability to shock. For some this may be affected by their background, others may do it unwittingly, whilst for others it may just be the fun of shocking adults and seeing their surprised faces. Be prepared!

Programme

The most important part of building a programme is deciding upon the aim. What is the one thing you want the children to remember when they get home? Having established that, all (or at least most) of the building blocks in the programme should stack up together around this aim.

Include variety and consistency. If it is the same every week it will be boring. If it is totally different each week, the children will appear lost and not really know what is going on. Children do appreciate routine.

Practical advice in constructing your programme

On pages 113 to 119 are some of the building blocks to include in a programme for this age group

Art and craft

Children usually enjoy making things but remember that their fine motor skills are still developing. A 7-year-old may find the activity a bit easy while the 5-year-old will need a good deal of help. This activity can include colouring, cutting, sticking, painting, modelling (clay or play dough), simple origami, collage.

There are advantages in doing a group exercise (such as a collage) that everyone can join in and can see displayed in the group area. But children also like to take home something that they have done to illustrate the aim or which might become a family treasure. Conversely an individual craft can reinforce the aim but may also mean that the children are more isolated from each other. So include both group and individual crafts.

Craft time is a great time for speaking and listening. Children love to chatter while they are working on a craft activity. Talk about their week, the aim of the session, what they like watching on the television or their favourite food.

Bible

The Bible must be the focal point of all we do, so it is important to use it whenever possible. Children will remember a positive experience of handling the Bible. If they learn how to handle it for themselves, however limited that may be for this age group, they will be equipped for life. The Bible will potentially be with them for life, long after all adults from the 5 to 7s group have gone. Aim to have at least one Bible visible and preferably open during the session. Your enthusiasm for the Bible will be infectious. Demonstrate that in the way you read it to the children and handle the book itself. Show them your Bible and where you are reading from. Of course, if you are reading the actual words of the Bible, it is essential to use an appropriate child-friendly version.

Encourage older and more able readers to read the Bible for themselves. You could use the Bible itself or print out a few verses, enlarged and laid out, so that they can draw expressions on blank faces, underline key or repeated phrases, or write or draw ideas in a thought bubble.

Chapter Link

Chapter 3 explores the development of children.
Chapter 7 explores the importance of using the Bible in more detail.

Cooking and sweet making

This is similar to craft but edible! Your facilities will affect what is possible. For example, you will need water for washing hands, a floor that can get messy and an oven nearby (or at home that you can use). Children this age love cooking, either making gifts for the family or more often simply food to be eaten. Many Bible stories naturally lead on to cooking or eating – bread and fish with feeding the 5,000 or the breakfast on the beach; a banquet in Luke 14 or a wedding in John 2; the feast after Ezra read the law in Nehemiah 8. Cooking provides time for talking with the children. You might learn something about how well (or poorly) you have communicated the aim for the session. Whether or not food is eaten will depend on the time of day, allergies and parental approval!

Dance

Most children of this age (especially at the younger end of the spectrum) enjoy dancing and movement.

- It may be free dance to some music to express themselves.
- It may be a liturgical dance that is choreographed.
- It may be with ribbons or flags (be extra careful with flag waving children – they can be quite dangerous).
- It may be part of a game.
- It may be part of an imaginative journey.

As we get older we lose some of the exuberance and joy that a child would naturally have. It is helpful for the children in our care to express themselves physically, boys included.

Drama and imagination

Most children play pretend games entering the world of their imagination. Drama makes use of this.

- You could present the Bible story as a drama.
- Children could re-enact at least part of the story (the animals going into the ark, different seed being scattered and growing up, Joseph's brothers squabbling!).
- Role play. Getting the children to put themselves in the position of one of the characters in the story.

Chapter Link

Chapters 3 and 4 give details of the opportunities for using drama and play in a church group as well as making the most of different learning styles. The value of speaking and listening is also explored.

Games

Some children love running around games, others prefer quieter, sitting down ones. This can vary from one part of the day to another. Children this age do a lot of learning through play. So include something of play or games in your programme. Sometimes you could play boisterous games that wear out the leaders as much as the children. At other times, play more sedentary games.

Games should be fun. We play them because we enjoy them. There don't have to be winners and losers. If this is handled carefully it should not present a problem. Occasionally you will be able to relate the games into the main theme. At other times you can play games just because they are fun and it is another way of getting to know your children better. Always be aware of children with any disabilities that will affect their ability to join in a games session.

Interviews with guests

Having visitors come to the group gives others the opportunity to see 'what really goes on' at your Sunday or midweek group. As appropriate invite guests to join you and where it fits into your programme ask them to share.

One church asked an elderly lady to join a group on Remembrance Sunday to talk about what it was like to live on rations. She even brought her ration book with her. Both she and the group enjoyed the experience.

Invite a baker (or someone who is into home baking) to talk about bread, both unleavened and leavened. What does yeast do?

Is there a fisherman in your church? How does his form of fishing differ from that of Peter, Andrew, James and John?

When you invite a guest in it is usually best to interview them. If you ask them to just speak about their subject they may dry up, go on too long or pitch what they say at the wrong age group. Prepare some questions in advance and talk them through with your guest before the session.

If you have time and your guest is brave enough, allow the children to ask questions. One blind person was interviewed by a group of 5 to 7s. They asked all kinds of logical, practical and insightful questions about her blindness. This allowed them to discover that when she eats she feels her food on her plate first and if it is fried egg, she gets yolk on her fingers!

Testimony is also a very powerful teaching medium. If one of the leaders (or a guest) can add a personal story or insight relating to their relationship with God it can help the children understand the reality of what is being said.

Memory

Most 5 to 7s have good memories, usually better than the memory of adults! So teach them verses from the Bible. You can do this in a variety of ways – using music, rhymes, actions, emphasising key words. Children also remember a phrase or song that sums up a theme that is being explored or practised. One very simple example: some children's clubs are called JAM club, JAM being short for Jesus and Me. That is a great way of helping children remember what a club is all about.

If you are teaching children a Bible verse:

- Use a suitable translation.
- Explain any difficult words or concepts and put the verse in its wider context.
- Make sure that it is relevant to their lives.
- Ask the question, will this verse help them when they are older? In other words, if they remember this verse in ten years time, will it serve to remind them of what they discovered about God when they were 5 to 7?
- Use different creative ways of exploring a memory verse such as arm and hand signs, hangman to sort out the letters, a rhyme or skipping rope, phrases hidden in a balloon which is then burst.

It is amazing how many older people still remember verses they learnt at Sunday School many years ago. The translation may be out of date and the language dated but the message lives on through memory.

Music and singing

- Music can be fun – especially if you choose the right songs. (Songs about just one idea, using appropriate non-jargon words with a singable tune are best!)
- Words and tunes often stay in children's minds for a long time.
- Children love rhythm and sound. Their world is full of sounds.
- Children love making music with instruments or by singing or shouting, accompanied by using their bodies to make suitable actions.
- Music can help all people worship God, and children are no exception. We must be careful not to put words into the mouths of children that they do not understand at all and maybe do not believe. Children who are already conscious of their relationship with God will want to tell him that they love him. But children who are from an unchurched background will not initially understand this. We need to be careful that we choose songs appropriate to the understanding and experience of the children that we have in our group.

Do not worry if you are not musical or there is not a musician in your team. If you can hold a tune (just listen to the song on the CD over and over again) then the children will follow you. Having things musically correct is far less important than enjoying yourself and learning through song. There are loads of music CDs available.

You can also make or purchase musical instruments: shakers, blowers and things to bang. These, properly supervised, will enhance your times of singing.

News or circle time

Most schools will have a time each week (or more regularly) when the children sit in a circle, pass around an object and the child holding the object can share some news. If you do this in your group, you may learn some interesting and helpful things about the children you are working with and they will learn from each other. You may not want to do this every week but as seems appropriate. This is also a good starting off point for encouraging children to pray for themselves and each other.

Offering

Children enjoy giving to others. There are plenty of opportunities to organise a fund-raising project for your group to get involved with.

It needs to be an integral part of your programme that is accompanied by what the Bible teaches broadly about giving and generosity.

The project needs to relate to children.

The target must be achievable.

Use pictures and updates to show the children what they are achieving.

Encourage the children to 'earn' the money themselves rather than just asking their parents for it.

An example might be raising enough money for a named child in Uganda to have basic school equipment or a named child in Peru to have regular meals. Many organisations run such projects. If you ask them they will be happy to supply you with ideas. Take a look at the following websites for organisations that have child sponsorship schemes: www.worldvision.org.uk, www.rope.org.uk, www.CompassionUK.org

Prayer

If we, as adults, appreciate the value of prayer it is vital that we encourage children to develop the habit at an early age. It is easy to slip into the bad habit of using prayer as a 'Lord we are here, please bless us' mantra. However, there is so much more we can do. Make sure you regularly spend quality time praying. Remember that speaking and listening is an important part of the child's development. What is prayer if it isn't speaking and listening?

Chapter Link

For more details on encouraging children to pray with God, turn to chapter 7.

Puppets

Most children of this age love puppets. Some people are very skilled at using puppets and develop the art of ventriloquism but there are other ways of using puppets.

- Build a simple puppet theatre – create or buy some scripts. This may take time but will prove beneficial.
- Use the puppets to sing songs from a CD.
- Use the puppet to whisper in your ear so that you do the talking rather than the puppet speaking.
- Children often identify with a puppet in a way that they cannot with an adult. They can say things to a puppet they might not say to an adult!
- A puppet cannot really have a relationship with God as it is only a puppet. Be careful what words you put into its mouth.

There are three important things to remember about using puppets.

- Practice, practice, practice. All good puppeteers spend a lot of time working with their puppets.
- Make sure the puppet keeps moving. As soon as it stops it loses life.
- Use the puppets as a means of applying what you are communicating, trying to earth your application into the lives of the children.

Quizzes

- A quiz can be just a fun game.
- A quiz that is based on general knowledge that is likely to be known by both churched and fringe children is a great way of showing acceptance of everyone.
- Children who are not good at quizzes hate them! A child who is hurt by a wrong answer may never return.
- Quizzes can take over the programme. A maximum of five questions for each side is reasonable to keep the programme moving.
- A question answered correctly may give the opportunity to ask supplementary questions to help explore the teaching of the session.

Use a quiz to remind children what they have already heard, either late in the programme to look back at what was learnt earlier or early in the next session to see what is remembered from the previous day or week. Questions can be true or false, multiple choice, individual or group response. Make sure children from an unchurched background or with a disability are not disadvantaged in any way.

Be creative and imaginative in the way that you score the quiz. You might choose to have the same teams each week and have an ongoing score or you might change the teams each week/session. The important thing is not the score or who wins and loses but the act of taking part to reinforce the theme. It is unwise to have boys versus girls at this age although some of the children may think that is a good idea.

Refreshments

Food and drink play an important part in all church life. So spend some of your time eating and drinking with the children. Fit it into the theme if at all possible. Most children love a party, so ensure you have some fun around eating. There are many imaginative ways of making food different and the children can always help prepare food. (See Cooking on page 114 earlier in this chapter.) Parents are often willing to help with food which is one way to involve parents on the fringe. Do not forget to check if children have allergies.

Stories

Telling stories, whether Bible stories or sharing your own personal story of what God means to you, will be an essential part of all you do. For ideas on storytelling turn to page 129 in chapter 7.

Discipline issues

Poor behaviour can begin for a multitude of reasons: learning difficulties, low self-image, slow development, a difficult home situation, lack of boundaries at home, the group's dynamic, a personality clash, the leader's lack of organisation and preparation. Here are a few pointers to help you address individual situations that occur in your group.

What doesn't work?

- Taking the poor behaviour personally – this can ultimately lead to a breakdown of relationship between the leader and child.
- Shouting all the time.
- Giving the attention-seeking child too much attention.
- Escalating the situation – take a step back.
- Being aggressive.
- Picking on one child, even if they are the most poorly behaved.
- Comparing children, especially siblings.
- Having favourites.

All of the above often happen because leaders are desperately trying to resolve a very difficult and complicated situation. However, these usually inflame the situation rather than resolve it.

What does work?

- Value each child. It is not always easy to remember that each child is made in the image of God and that he loves them. If a child is valued by God, we should show how much we value them.
- Reward good behaviour.
- Build good ongoing relationships between leaders and children. Be positive and encouraging. Get to know your children.
- Prepare well as the leader.
- Pray for the children, before, during and after the session and pray in the room for the children before they arrive.
- Be first there, be organised and welcome each child with a smile.
- Make the children feel accepted in the group by speaking positively to them.
- Use a child's name as often as possible.
- Give clear and specific instructions to the group or an individual.
- Where possible offer choices.
- Use your voice wisely. It is a great tool – know when to whisper, when to be calm, when to be more severe.
- Form good relationships with parents.
- Affirm and acknowledge genuine improvements.

Setting up a policy or procedure

- Children need discipline, routine and structure to make sense of their world.

List of rules for handling difficult behaviour

1. Try to get agreement (or at least understanding of why the rules are there) from the children. Ownership of them is important.

2. Use positive language.

3. Praise the children when they work within the boundaries that have been laid down.

4. Choose to operate a reward system but this can create problems with some children feeling that they are left out and others favoured.

5. Decide (early on) what happens if someone continually breaks the rules. Whatever you decide you need to stick to it and follow through with it. (You may want to think about a chill out area or somewhere the child can find space for a period of time.) Remember that physical punishment or cutting words are not appropriate and should not be used.

6. Any consequences should be appropriate, thought through in advance, if possible positive and carried out.

7. Be patient and consistent; do not increase or change the consequences just because a child has really annoyed you.

8. Reward and encourage positive behaviour.

Chapter Link

Chapter 3 explores the development of children.

- Consider what makes a good rule. It should be clear, relevant, achievable, understood, fair and clearly communicated.
- Agree (if possible with the children involved in the process) on a list of rules. Keep this as simple as possible. Write the rules up and display them for all to see.

When it comes to discipline it is helpful to keep in mind that it is the poor behaviour that we dislike not the child. It is worth asking who is the behaviour a problem for and what exactly is the problem? Is there a pattern of behaviour? When does the problem occur? Where does it occur? Is there a trigger to the behaviour? How might the situation be resolved?

Top Tips on Handling difficult behaviour
Graham Finch

A practical and encouraging guide for all those seeking to disciple children effectively. Explore some of the reasons for bad behaviour and the common mistakes we make in dealing with it. Find out how to take control and enlist your group's help in making your times together enjoyable for all – including you!
ISBN 978 1 84427 124 5
£2.99

Craft books resources

Activities for All Year Round		Usborne
Amazing Art Attack Stuff	Neil Buchanan	Dorling Kindersley
Art Attack: Even More Cool Stuff	Neil Buchanan	Dorling Kindersley
Chocolates and Sweets to Make		Usborne
Christmas Things to Stitch and Sew		Usborne
Easter Cooking		Usborne
Easter Things to Make and Do		Usborne
50 Rainy Day Activities		Usborne
50 Science Things to Make and Do		Usborne
50 Things to Draw and Paint		Usborne
Here's Another One I Made Earlier	Kathryn Copsey	Scripture Union
Here's One I Made Earlier	Kathryn Copsey	Scripture Union
I Can Make Starry Things for Christmas	Jocelyn Miller	Lion Hudson
Look What I Made	Christina Goodings	Lion Hudson
My Christmas Crafts	Anna Murray, Linda Watts	Salamander
Origami and other Paper Projects		Usborne
Things to Make and Do for Christmas		Usborne
30 Things to Cook and Eat for Christmas		Usborne

Chapter 7 – Inspirational ideas

Working with 5 to 7s has many great joys, not least of which is being able to enter into the worlds created by their vivid imaginations. Put most children of this age in a room with a table, a sheet and a large cardboard box and watch them invent endless places, events and activities full of colour, detail and excitement! It is a privilege and education to be invited to be part of their play.

When Jacob was 5 years and 5 weeks old his parents served on a Scripture Union summer activity team. There was a period of about 45 minutes each day when both parents were tied up with important tasks, so one of the other team members would play with Jacob. In no time at all he had organised her to throw a duvet over the bunk beds and so transform them into a tent, inside which he loved to play card games such as 'Pairs' or simply just chat. He would search around for everyday items that could be commandeered and put to good use: a tube of hand cream became the scanner at a supermarket checkout. When his 'customer' apologised that she did not have enough money to pay for the goods at this impromptu shop he reassured her at once. 'It's alright, we take plastic!'

At the age of 7 years and 49 weeks, Jacob would be happily amused for the same length of time with a sheet of A4 paper, with which he would invent and create games. His mind teemed with ideas and through the years from being just 5 to almost 8 he would never be bored if left to play alone for a while, because he could always think of something to do with the minimum of equipment.

It is our joy – and sometimes our struggle – to interact with children like Jacob and to find ways of stretching their minds to help them grow in their relationship with God and their knowledge of him. So our methodology needs to be varied and we need to give them scope for their imagination to assist in this vital task. But they may be in a group alongside others who are very different and who seem dull at the side of these bright, creative thinkers. We have to meet the needs of all the children, and help each one to know God, and his love for them.

Using the Bible

Laura, aged 6, had enjoyed hearing about Jesus at a Scripture Union summer event and so was very excited when she bought a Bible from the bookstall. Clutching her new treasure she announced to her group leader, 'Next year I'm going to buy a different Bible so I can read all the other stories about Jesus!'

The Bible is so important in helping children to know God and to discover what it means to walk with Jesus through life! Some children recognise that themselves. A survey of 5- to 7-year-olds asked what helped them to get to know Jesus better, and almost half the children gave the answer 'the Bible' without any prompting from an adult. And yet it is far from being

Resources

Big Bible Story Book

978 1 84427 228 0 £12.99

Re-told Bible stories, with photographic illustration, from Genesis to Revelation for very young children and their parents to enjoy together.

Join in, jump on! (6 titles)

£2.99 each

Undated booklets to help early readers develop a relationship with God – Bible verses to read, simple activities and prayer suggestions for every day.

The Red Book of Must Know stories
The Green Book of Must Know stories
by Alexander Brown £2.99

After a survey ten Bible stories were selected as the ten key ones to be passed onto the next generation – the Must Know stories. These ten stories, published by Scripture Union in 2008, are for three target audiences – 5 to 7s, 8 to 11s and adults. The 5 to 7s stories are in two books and are a Must Have. For more details visit www.scriptureunion.org.uk

Look out for *Top Tips: Sharing Bible stories*. See page 133 for details

Quotes about Bible from children

5-7s year olds were asked this question: What would you invent to help other children explore the Bible? Here's their reply:

Chewing gum and chews with a Bible verse on them when chewed.

Invent a big machine/robot, press a button and it would tell you a Bible story.

A bag to always carry a small Bible.

A special Bible club to tell children about it all.

Make a proper phone to talk with Jesus – an interactive chat with God!

a simple book to read, especially for young children. They need as much help as possible. Here are some ways to enable them to read it and get to know its truths.

- Use a suitable translation. Several modern ones, such as the *Contemporary English Version*, the *Good News Bible* and the *International Children's Bible* are useful with children but they will still be hard for this age group. The vocabulary used is too wide and sentence formation is often too complex. Children who have enjoyed one of the many versions suitable for toddlers may well struggle to make the leap into these translations. Bible story books bridge the gap between the 'few words, many pictures' of Bibles for under 5s and full Bibles that are the complete reverse.
- Help them to grasp that this is God's book, written a very long time ago, but which is still true today. It helps us to know God better and to understand more about God the Father, Jesus his son, and the Holy Spirit, as well as showing us what it means to be Jesus' friend.
- Help them to understand the difference between life in Bible times and now. There are a number of good books that will help you to do this, such as *The Children's Guide to the Bible* or *Bible Alive* (both Scripture Union).
- Set Bible passages in a time context. Again, many adults struggle with the fact that the Bible is not arranged chronologically, and children of this age will not have a clue whether Elijah came before or after Jesus, never mind before or after Elisha. To them 'the olden days' stretch from the time the world began to just before they were born! Having a grasp of God's faithfulness over generations is important, so they do need to know stories from both Old and New Testaments.
- Differentiate between different types of writing. Many adults never grasp the fact that the Bible contains a number of styles of text, and that the type of writing has a bearing on our understanding of it. Is everything in the Bible written for everyone at all times? Check out Paul's instructions to Timothy in 1 Timothy 5:23 if you are unsure! (Timothy had a personal physical problem which Paul addressed. Is his advice for all time, only for people with stomach problems or only for Timothy's case!?)

At 5 children cannot differentiate between made-up story and actual events retold, let alone between history and prophecy. But if taught the differences, they will begin to understand. Even if they are only beginning to grasp that the Bible contains both stories of things that actually happened (history) and stories that were made up to help people understand God (eg parables), it is important that we understand the difference as we teach them. We do not want them to have to 'unlearn' anything in later life.

Readers may benefit from having the Bible passage retyped in a larger font and placed alone on a page. It is far less daunting to read five lines of normal print on a sheet of paper than to read ten short lines in tiny print, buried amongst lots of others that look just the same. When asked what she would invent to help children explore the Bible Rachel, aged 6, astutely said, 'Bigger writing'!

- Choose passages with care. Not everything in the Bible is suitable for children and we need to be wise in our selection of material. Some passages never feature in children's

Q: I wonder which bit you like best...
A: Leading on the paths

Psalm 23

You, Lord, are my shepherd. I will never be in need. You let me rest in fields of green grass. You lead me to streams of peaceful water, and you refresh my life. You are true to your name, and you lead me along the right paths.

I may walk through valleys as dark as death, but I won't be afraid. You are with me, and your shepherd's rod makes me feel safe.

You treat me to a feast, while my enemies watch. You honour me as your guest, and you fill my cup until it overflows.

Your kindness and love will always be with me each day of my life, and I will live for ever in your house, Lord.

Q: I wonder how you'd feel as a sheep, being looked after by this shepherd...

A: Good. You wouldn't have to find your own food

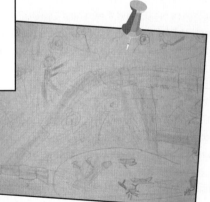

Q: I wonder how it makes you feel...
A: Like I was dreaming I was in that place

material for good reason! Stories such as that of Jephthah (Judges 11:30–40), the man who foolishly made a vow to sacrifice to God whatever came out of his house when he arrived home in triumph (only to be greeted by his daughter!) may be inappropriate for children of this age. Whilst older ones might see the stupidity of Jephthah's vow, children of this age will take the story at face value and are more likely to be frightened by it. The account of Samuel being left at the temple by his mother (1 Samuel 1) may strike fear in the heart of a 5-year-old. I have heard a very skilled, sensitive and well thought-out retelling of the narrative of Abraham. The speaker explained how Abraham was willing to sacrifice his young son, Isaac, followed by the comment that God will never again ask a father to do that to his child. However many would simply avoid it at this age. It is far better to do that than to tell it in a way that causes anxiety.

Some children, especially boys, will relish stories that contain a gory element, and enjoy the Bible more for hearing narratives that are not just 'nice'. But use them with great care. We need to know our children well so that we choose the right narratives. Our aim is to inspire, not to scare! Maybe parents can take more risks than church children's workers.

Helen says: 'Some would say that children of this age should not be taught about the crucifixion. I believe that without it, the gospel is watered down to nothing more than Jesus being a good and kind person, and so it must be taught – but with caution. They do not need to know details of nails and swords, just basic truths: 'Jesus the Son of God never did anything wrong, but he was killed on a cross.'

Ian was 5 when he watched a simple video retelling the crucifixion. As it drew to a close he turned to his group leader with wide eyes. 'Claire,' he said, 'Jesus died!'
7-year-old Christopher reacted similarly, going home from the club to tell his mother all about it. His father, a vicar, said that whilst Christopher had heard the story before, on this occasion the reality of it had made sense in his head and was lodged in his heart.
Use some of the storytelling techniques below to enhance Bible stories. Make them memorable and exciting, help the children to enter into them and apply them to the children's lives as and when appropriate.

In earlier chapters we touched on circle time, where children sit and listen to one another and talk about important issues. This works very well with Bible passages as it gives every child an opportunity to contribute comments, ask questions and explore the story in more depth. It does not matter one bit if they all say much the same thing. The activity gives them an opportunity to talk about the Bible and to grow in confidence.

The fact that a 5-year-old cannot yet read fluently should not stop us reading the Bible with them individually. Read them a Bible story and then talk about it; time spent talking about the Bible with a parent, grandparent, carer or church children's leader will increase their confidence to read and understand God's word. As the Bible itself says, 'Memorize (God's) laws and tell them to your children over and over again. Talk about them all the time, whether

Story-telling advice

Look through the suggestions on the following pages and consider how you might use them as you tell stories.

Verbal techniques

Your voice is your most important tool in good storytelling. Speak clearly and project your voice (do not shout!) if you have a large group of children. Seek the help of a speech and language therapist if you do not know how to project your voice and are using storytelling with any regularity.

Volume. Speak in the most normal volume possible at which you can be heard, so that you can add in the other techniques effectively.

Pitch. Speaking at a normal pitch will be more comfortable on the children's ears and better for your voice, but use occasional changes to denote the voices of different characters.

Pace. Increase it to give a sense of urgency or excitement; slow it down to describe a tired person's journey, or to build suspense.

Intonation. Stress appropriate words (usually adjectives) to build a picture. So, for example, have an 'enormous' crowd listening to Jesus talking (5,000 is meaningless to children of this age) or talk about the 'wonderful' sense of excitement and amazement for Mary when she recognised Jesus after he came alive.

Accents. If you can achieve a variety of accents then you might use them to differentiate between characters. But they do need to be different enough from each other for the children to tell who is speaking and they do need to be used consistently! A story told well in the same accent is better than one told less well by a variety of voices.

you're at home or walking along the road or going to bed at night, or getting up in the morning.' (Deuteronomy 6:6,7) At the older end of the age group, use published materials that give a short passage to be read and follow it with simple questions or puzzles. Be ready for the fact that conversation will not be simplistic. Reading together like this will raise all kinds of issues – and opportunities!

Storytelling

Children are well used to listening to stories together as a group in school. The fortunate ones will also enjoy the intimacy of sitting cuddled up with their parent, where it is perhaps easier to inhabit the world of the story and be fully immersed in it. Not every child is good at listening and distractions will always pull the attention of some in the group (usually boys) from the words they hear, so we need to work hard on techniques that make the stories we tell as exciting, interesting and riveting as possible.

There are a number of very useful books on storytelling that will help you think through the process and teach you techniques in far more detail than can be covered here, but the following points will help.

Creating stories

You may want to create a story rather than read someone else's. If so, consider the following:
- Appropriateness. Is it appropriate for:
  Children of this age? Does it include concepts that are beyond their concrete thinking?
  Their backgrounds and culture?
  The truth you are trying to convey?
- Repetition: the rule of 3. For some reason, repeating a word twice seems to work much better than once! Three has a sense of wholeness about it. 'Up, up, up the tree climbed Zacchaeus' gives a sense of the height he needed to reach to see over people's heads.
- Realism. Use realistic situations, characters and names. When you were young it was likely that every child to appear in a preacher's story was called 'Little Johnny'. Use reality and variety in naming people, at least for the sake of boys called Johnny!
- Brevity. Keep it as short as possible!

Using non-Bible stories to teach Bible truths

Jesus used the ordinary things of life to draw people's attention, and set his stories in their world. So when teaching the crowds he talked about family life, farming and other familiar activities, explaining the deep truths of the Kingdom of God through everyday images. As our aim is to help children to grow in their knowledge of and relationship with God we want to make his word and his truths as accessible as possible to them.

We need to be careful not to confuse children by mixing stories so that they think Little Nutbrown Hare was on Noah's ark. I once heard a man ask his 5-year-old granddaughter if she had heard the story of Jesus' birth at school. 'Yes,' she said, 'Mary and Jesus and Snow White!' We need to exercise caution and explain the difference clearly, but the stories they know from home or school can often be used to illustrate Bible truths. Stories like Sam

Non-verbal techniques

Eye contact. Even if you are somewhat glued to the text because you are reading the story, use occasional eye contact to help keep the children's attention. Should any child become involved in distracting behaviour, a strong look may well stop them without you having to pause in the story or say anything about it.

Facial expressions. Your face should match any emotions being expressed in the story. It would be completely wrong to talk about Jesus dying on the cross whilst grinning from ear to ear. But similarly it enhances the impact if you smile with delight as you talk about him coming alive again.

Gestures. Emphasise words (usually verbs) by gestures, such as arms open in welcome when the father first sees his prodigal son, or a foot that stamps defiance when the elder son is angry that his brother has been welcomed home.

Posture and body language. If you have a small group of children, stay seated at a level close to theirs so that you can maintain eye contact. For larger groups you may want to stand or even walk about, but make sure that they can follow you with their eyes and that your movement does not detract from the story.

Sounds. Some sound effects could add to the story but choose carefully. Or appropriate music played quietly in the background can enhance the mood of a story.

Smells. You might spray some perfume when telling about the lady who poured perfume over Jesus' feet, or simply ask the children to imagine what they would smell if they were in the story. You may get over reactions and silliness if you ask them to imagine the smell, say, of the lions' den in which Daniel spent the night, so choose carefully!

Taste. Food makes stories much more memorable! Do check that all the group can eat the food; beware excluding children who have allergies to certain foods.

Visuals. Use pictures (in a book and held up for the children to see, drawn large on card, or projected via PowerPoint or an overhead projector). They can be 'Biblical' pictures or you may find a contemporary photograph that meets the need. Sometimes at the start of a club session with children I have had them paint in large outlines of pictures that tell a particular story, and then these have been used to illustrate the story. The children have loved seeing their pictures used this way! Or hold up objects that relate to the story and help to focus their attention. Use visuals that are big enough for the size of your group; an A4 picture will not work in a school hall, but a large picture will still be fine with three or four children.

Costumes. Either dress up yourself or have children dressed in appropriate costumes while you narrate the story.

McBratney's *Guess How Much I Love You* and *You're All My Favourites* and Debbie Gliori's *No Matter What* illustrate something of what the Bible says about God's love. When they hear the story again, children may remember this truth as well. The story of *Dogger* by Shirley Hughes tells of a much loved toy dog that is lost, and when next seen it has been bought by another child at a jumble sale. The toy is finally restored to the child who loves him so much by exchange. Not all the details fit, but there are definite echoes of what God has done for us through Jesus!

Video, DVD and storytelling

Not everyone feels comfortable or capable of telling stories to children and there are lots of videos and DVDs that provide useful alternatives. It is not ideal to use these every week, not least because many children spend a lot of time at home watching television. So it is a joy and wonder for them to have an adult telling a story.

Some things to consider when choosing and using these media:
• Is the retelling accurate to the Bible?
• Is it appropriate for the age of the children?
• Do you have adequate equipment for the task – eg can the children see and hear clearly enough?
• Does the film keep the children's attention adequately?
• Do the children listen well and take in the information from the film?
• If you have children who struggle to sit still through a story, or who have behaviour problems, how will you accommodate their needs? One of the advantages of a 'live' storyteller is that they can pause momentarily and say, 'Sit down please, Ryan!' and continue with the story! A DVD cannot do that, and the children may miss something while an adult says 'Sit down please, Ryan!' over the soundtrack.

Godly play

In our zeal to help children meet with God through his word we sometimes tell them exactly what we think a passage or story means and in doing so direct the interaction between the child and God. Jerome Berryman, a theologian and priest in the USA, has created a methodology known as Godly play that allows children to discover their own understanding of Scripture by interacting with the narrative through play. Linked to this, the adult leader will pose very open questions, often beginning with the words 'I wonder...' This style of learning uses simple wooden figures to tell Bible stories. The children can then play with the figures themselves, retelling the story and becoming familiar with it. There is a relatively slow pace to the storytelling and the style encourages reflection as the story progresses. A number of other techniques are used that enhance the children's entry into and involvement in the story, such as the fact that the storyteller does not make eye contact with the children but focuses attention on the figures being used, so drawing the child's focus into the story.

To use Godly play to its full effect you will need to go on an accredited course, details of which are available in the resources section at the end of this chapter.

Involvement

Have the children mime the story as you tell it. Dress them up and put them in place to form a tableau, or tell the story twice, getting the children to mime it the second time having first heard the story.

You could ask them to join in or respond to certain words in the story. For example, they might say 'baa' whenever you say the word 'sheep', or stand up, turn round and sit down whenever you say the word 'go!' However opinion is divided on this: whilst some like this as a way of involving children, others feel that the children are then just listening out for that word, rather than listening to the story. What may work better is to hold up simple cue cards of words such as 'Wow!' to be said at the appropriate moment. Remember to tell them what the word is before you begin the story, for the benefit of those who struggle with reading.

Application. If you are going to apply a story to the children's lives, think carefully about it first.

How? Is it appropriate:

- for the children in the group?
- for their age?
- for the passage or story?
- for your learning objectives?

When? Again, opinion is divided on this. Traditionally the application has come after the story – 'here's the story and now this is what it means' – but it is astonishing how quickly children will 'switch off' from listening once a story has ended! So it may work better to apply the story before you tell it, and then reiterate the application, or to explain it just before the story ends. To do so needs careful thought so that it comes in the right place – while the children are still waiting for the outcome of events, but where it does not detract from the storyline.

Of course there is another school of thought that says stories should not be interpreted or applied, but the children should be left to work it out for themselves. The example is given of Jesus telling parables and leaving them with 'those who have ears to hear', although he was talking with adults. But many people would say that a story 'gets inside' its listeners and needs to be allowed to remain and work in them uncluttered by the opinions of others.

Look out for *Top tips: Sharing Bible stories. Inspirational ideas, practical advice and real life stories to help you share Bible stories with your children's group.* Published in April 2008.

Godly play is a useful tool to aid us in bringing the Bible alive to children. Even if you do not want to be trained in this technique there are lessons for us in using this open style of questioning from time to time. It allows children to make up their own minds and tell you what they think, rather than suggesting to them that there is one right answer and no scope for difference of opinion or insight.

Prayer

We want children to have a balanced view of God: to have a sense of him as the creator and sustainer of the universe who is holy and just, but that he's someone who is closer than their best friend, more willing to listen and talk with them than even their parents, and whose love for them is the greatest they will ever experience. So we want children to be comfortable with prayer. Our desire is for them to talk with God about anything and everything, about their hopes and fears, their frustrations and disappointments or their desires for their families, friends and the wider world in which they live.

The hymn *Lord, teach us how to pray!* by James Montgomery, written in the 19th century expresses the view that:

> 'Prayer is the simplest form of speech
> That infant lips can try.'

It is a sentiment that may seem far from reality as you try to help young children to distinguish between what they want God to do this week for Granny who is very poorly, and what they want Father Christmas to bring them at the end of the year. The two may easily become muddled! Prayer can take many forms and it does not all have to be serious, spoken with closed eyes and tightly clasped hands, nor even be just about speaking to God.

At its essence, prayer is about building a friendship between the child and God. The problem of not being able to see God may confuse some, especially those who have imaginary friends. What is the difference? Just as their regular conversation – albeit sometimes silent – with an imaginary friend means that they are able to tell you what the friend is thinking, saying and doing, so these children may have no difficulty in chatting with God. But we must teach them that he is real.

I suspect that many adults are shy about praying out loud in a group of people because they are afraid they will get the words wrong or 'not pray a good enough prayer'. They are not worried about God's opinion, but are concerned about what others in the group will think if they are not fluent, fail to use long words or if their prayer is not 'spiritual enough'. Thankfully young children are generally free from such hang-ups and praying with them will doubtless increase our confidence as well as theirs! Unlike adults they will not rehearse the prayer in their heads and then be devastated if the person before them prays the same thing. They may say 'He said my prayer!' with a degree of indignation but will then happily go on to say it themselves once told that a repeat is fine.

Prayers

Dear God

Sorry for not listening when I have been naughty. Amen

Connor age 6

Dear God

When my friends are poorly please make them better. Amen

Elizabeth age 5

How

- Children are often encouraged to pray with their eyes closed and hands together as an aid to concentration. After all, as a wise infant teacher once said, 'Do you know how many exciting things you can do with eight fingers and two thumbs during a few moments of silence?' Here are some alternative 'eyes open' activities that may help concentration.
- Use pictures that illustrate the prayer's content.
- Give children objects to hold in their hands that link in to the prayer's theme.
- Use large cards with words on them such as 'Wow!', 'Thanks', 'Please', 'Sorry' and 'Shhhhh…' to help focus the children's minds on the prayer.
- Make a flip-over book of pictures and words taking children through the Lord's Prayer that both remind them of the words and help to explain its meaning.
- Church House Publishing has produced The Lord's Prayer Cube, a hinged wooden block that unfolds to show the different parts of the prayer in picture form. It may be especially helpful to children who are unused to church and therefore not familiar with the prayer.
- Have the children come out and put their hands on a globe when praying for countries or problems around the world. The bigger it is the better! If you cannot do this, have a world map to show where the countries are. They can still come and lay hands on the map.
- Give some background information that helps the child to understand what it is like to live there – eg 'It's hot and people get very tired when they have to carry water. They can't just turn on a tap – they have to walk as far as from here to your school just to get a drink of water!'
- Use a PowerPoint presentation or pictures on an OHP during church services to help the children to understand what you are praying for. See the final section of this chapter for some practical tips on using these media in worship with 5 to 7s.

What

- The youngest of this age group especially may struggle with thinking of topics for prayer. Ask for suggestions of what you should pray about, but be prepared to direct their thinking a little. 5-year-olds will still be bound up in their world, with the things they know about. Help them to think wider.
- Show appropriate photographs from the newspapers or magazines. Then talk about the different issues that need prayer.
- Help them to imagine what it must be like for the people in those situations. 'What does this lady look like?' Sad. 'Why do you think she is sad?' Because her son has gone off to fight in the war. 'What could we pray for her?' That her son will come home soon. That he won't be hurt. As you involve their imaginations as to what is happening in the situations for which you are praying they will have a better understanding of these people's needs. It will take them (and you) to a deeper level of prayer.
- Create a 'prayer book' for regular topics with photographs of people – such as the church staff team, any mission partners, people in the community known to the children (local school staff, community police, crossing attendants, etc) or names of people who

The Lord's Prayer Cube

This delightful, full-colour and robust cube is an ideal way to help 4 to 8s engage with the Lord's Prayer – to be used in the home or church context. For more details visit www.chpublishing.co.uk

are ill long-term.

- Circle prayers. We want to give children confidence to pray so they may benefit from help with content. Sit everyone in a circle and explain first about what sort of prayer it will be (thanks, sorry, please, wow! etc). Give the children a moment to think of something for which they want to pray and then go round the circle asking what those things are. Finally lead them in prayer. Begin it, and then say something such as 'Especially we ask you to help these people…' and then go round the circle again for each child to say the name or event they thought of. Finally end it in an appropriate way and say 'Amen'. You could do the same with the children praying full prayers. If some children are not comfortable praying out loud then pass round a small object that can be held in the hand; children can either pray out loud or sit quietly holding the object while they pray in their heads, before passing it on to the next person.

Types of prayer
Telling God he is great
Adults would call this praise or adoration, and we are not always very good at it as our own 'shopping lists' sometimes overwhelm us and we lose sight of how amazing God is. Children may struggle to think of words but do have a sense of God's 'wow!' factor. It might be helpful to write the word 'wow!' and make the 'o' look like a mouth that is wide open with amazement. The prayer might be led by an adult with each section ending with the words, 'Lord God, you're really…' and the children join in with 'wow!' as you hold up the word.

Thanking God
- Ask children what they want to thank God for. They will usually have lots to say! It will feel a little like 'news time' and will probably gather momentum as time goes on, so be patient. If slow to start they may benefit from you saying what you want to thank God for. This will set them thinking and give them confidence.
- Get them to look out of a window and thank God for the things they can see that they appreciate.
- Give them a range of photographs from magazines, or some pictures of people known to them.
- Have them draw pictures of the people or things for which they want to say thank you. If they are very shy they only need to hold up the pictures!

Asking God
It never ceases to amaze me what children of this age will ask God for! Start the ball rolling and you could well be praying for hamsters that have poorly legs, rabbits that have had babies and a host of other kinds of veterinary problems. Perhaps this is because these things are very precious to them; it may also be that they are somewhat shielded from the important issues in family life and therefore are blissfully unaware that Uncle Bob is terminally ill and Daddy is about to be made redundant for the third time in 18 months. It is vital that we pray for the things they say, however trivial they may seem, because they matter to the children and the children matter to God. These issues may seem trifling to us compared to the problems of the world but I believe that it is in trusting God with the well-being of their much-loved pets that they both discover how to trust him for the really big things, and learn how much he loves them. But children at this age are just as capable of praying for big things and

Templates to use with prayer ideas

Please

Shhhhh.....

Sorry

Thanks

Wow

having the faith that God will answer positively.

Saying sorry

Use of this word is an important part of maintaining relationships. Soon after speech develops children are taught to say 'sorry' when they hurt someone. Of course the apology is made to the person who has been hurt and forgiveness is offered in return from the sister whose painting has been torn, the mother who has to clean up the mess when food is thrown in a tantrum, or the friend who has a ball snatched from them. As Christians we recognise that the things we do, say or think that are wrong hurt not just the people involved but God, too. In Psalm 51, we read of King David's remorse after his adultery with Bathsheba and his request for her husband to be placed in the heat of the battle so that he is killed. But his confession to God includes the words, 'You are really the one I have sinned against; I have disobeyed you and have done wrong.' (Psalm 51:4). Uriah, husband of Bathsheba, might have disagreed had he been alive to do so! The Christian faith recognises that when we do wrong to another person we also wrong God, and so we confess these things to him, too, and seek his forgiveness. But that does not make much sense to a young child. So keep 'sorry' prayers to a minimum at this age. As one diocesan children's adviser has pointed out, children who are present during the first part of a Church of England service are often only there long enough to tell God how bad they are!

Listening prayer

Most of us are better at talking than listening, especially where prayer is concerned. Silence may feel uncomfortable, and many adults will feel uncertain as to whether they truly hear God or are simply making up answers in their head. None of this is a good reason to avoid having 'listening prayer' with children from time to time.

Active prayer

Use activities such as making paper chains with prayers written on them about people today who are slaves; pinning 'sorry' prayers onto a cross; drawing pictures or writing prayers on two large hands: one to pray for people who are ill and the other for those who take care of them and work to make them well again. See the resource section for published materials that will give you lots of ideas.

Answers to prayers

To avoid the sense of speaking into a vacuum it is important to teach children that God does answer prayers, and to help them understand in what ways. You might use the symbol of traffic lights to explain this. See opposite.

Worship

There was quiet music playing in the room as children moved from one prayer activity to another. Some had dropped pebbles into the water to remind them that when God forgives, it is as if the wrong that we have done is washed away. Others had written prayers on fish shapes that were then placed in a net. More than one hundred 5 to 7s had moved quietly from one prayer station to another for the past ten minutes, and the music had provided a calm background to their activities. 7-year-old Joanna began to dance to it. None of the leaders prompted her – nor, thankfully, told her to stop. There was no sense of her showing off. This was Joanna's way of praising God.

Traffic lights answers to prayer

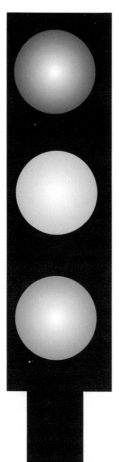

Red stands for 'no'. Explain that God is wise and knows what is best for us and others. Grown-ups sometimes say 'no' to things that we think would be great (ice cream and chocolate for every meal) because they know it would not be good for us. God makes those wise decisions too.

Amber shows just before the lights go green but means 'not yet'. There are times when it seems as if God is not answering our prayers but in fact he has answered with 'it's not yet time for the answer'. Time is not an easy concept for five-year-olds but older ones will understand better the idea of waiting for an answer.

Green stands for 'yes'.

Sam is energetic and cannot sit still for long. In church he loves songs that have a strong beat and he is now practising hard on the African drum that his dad bought for him. Steve, who plays drums in the worship band, is his role model. He has told Sam that you can worship God through drumming, which Sam thinks is great!

Anna is a lively 6-year-old who likes to be in the thick of everything. She is not especially fond of singing in church, but when someone offers flags to be waved she is usually the first to fetch one and swings it around enthusiastically.

Paul is a quiet 7-year-old who thinks deeply. He is good at writing and his favourite way to worship God is to write a poem or prayer. His poems often reflect something of the countryside in which he lives.

Children enjoy as many ways of worshipping God as adults do – probably more, in fact! Use a whole range of activities – songs, prayers, Bible input, active participation, listening, looking, a short time of reflection with some idea of what to think about and some way of responding. Choose songs with easy melodies, a good sense of rhythm, suitable words and preferably that cover a single concept (eg 'Our God is a great big God'). If you use actions keep them simple and appropriate for the words. Help children to join in but do not force them; at the age of 5, when co-ordination skills are still developing, it can be very hard to keep up with others who are more dextrous.

All this is so much easier to achieve when the worship is just for this age group! Do take time with those who lead worship for all ages, helping them to understand the children and enable them to enjoy what helps them to worship God.

Multimedia and worship

An increasing number of churches are using a multimedia approach in worship, with songs and liturgy being presented on a screen rather than as a book to hold. Music and spoken words are amplified, so it may not be obvious who is speaking at a given time. It can be hard for younger children to keep up with what is happening, and where. Here are some simple but practical tips to help children engage with worship in this form.

- Encourage those who sit with them to help children know where to look.
- Ask those leading worship to point to the screen and direct children's attention to any images there.
- Invite children to sit in places where they have better sight of a screen. This may not necessarily mean sitting at the front! As screens are usually placed high up children may be craning their necks in order to see words or images.
- Make good use of these media to involve children more – perhaps by putting pictures alongside text in liturgy or prayers; for quizzes or activities; showing simple words that sum up the main points of a talk; perhaps even displaying the children's own artwork for prayers of praise and thanks.

In general, if it helps children to be more engaged in worship, it will probably help adults too, so be creative and make the best use of technology!

Child-friendly prayer chart

On	We asked God ...	On	God answered ...
13th January	Help us with spelling test	14th January	We weren't nervous in the spelling test
	Keep Tom's Dad safe while away	16th January	Tom's Dad came home safe
20th January	Make Sarah's Gran better	26th January	Sarah's Gran died
	Help Josh at the dentist's this afternoon	20th January	Josh was fine at the dentist's
27th January	Help Sarah and her family when they are upset about her Gran	28th January	Sarah was OK at her Gran's funeral
		2nd February	Sarah enjoyed planting a rose to remember her Gran
	Help people to share food so there's enough in the world		

Chapter 8 – Children and Church

One way and another, Joe has spent quite a large proportion of his 6 years of life in church. As his parents attend their local church regularly Joe was first taken there when he was just a few days old. His mum also went to the toddler group each week and as Joe grew older and more active he and his father went to the 'Dads only' toddler session held twice each term on a Saturday morning. The family are usually at church early on a Sunday as Joe's dad helps with some of the jobs that need doing before the service begins, and as his parents have a lot of friends there they chat for quite a while after the service. Joe is very happy during these times as he, too, has friends there and they love playing together, even if it is just looking at each other's latest toy cars.

But how much does Joe feel part of what goes on between these enjoyable play times? In Chapter 1, we considered how the church views Joe and other children of his age. Here, we think about church from their perspective and look at some of the issues that go with being a 5-, 6- or 7-year-old in church.

All-age worship

Whether it is for ten minutes at the start of a service or for a short time at the end, most children attending church will be involved in worship with the adult congregation at some point on most Sundays. Once a month many will be part of an all-age worship service. As people who understand and work with 5- to 7-year-olds we may be asked to help with this or even to lead parts of the service. If what is planned goes way over the heads of the children week after week we should certainly be prepared to talk with those who plan and lead all-age worship whatever our role is in the upfront leading of such services.

On the opposite page you will find some characteristics of good all-age worship that help children to engage and be involved.

Of course children at this age have a sense of awe and wonder and so can cope with the need to be quiet at times, perhaps to focus on something such as a lighted candle (it will help if this is relatively close) but they will also appreciate things being quite matter of fact. Whilst we want them to discover something of God's majesty and glory, we also want them to know him as their loving Father who is ever-present.

Helen says: 'Two all-age services that I have attended stand out for me. At the first there was a friendly buzz as I arrived and people actually made eye contact and smiled in greeting to visitors who sat near them. The songs were short, lively and had good words that gave adults something to think about, yet were easily understood by a 5-year-old. The service included a brief explanation about the forthcoming gift day by the treasurer (who asked the children to consider what they could give), a Bible reading and well-illustrated talk in which assistance was given by a 7-year-old, and the baptism of a child whose twin had died at birth, which was

All-age worship

Hannah held her mother's hand as they left church one Sunday morning. She was so glad to be outside at last! The visiting preacher had gone on for a very long time and the three children who attend the small village chapel have to stay in throughout the service as there are neither leaders for a children's group nor any place where one can be held. They had finished their activity sheets and read the Bible story books provided for them long before the service came to an end. Hannah had been wriggling and restless for the last half hour of the service. Hannah's mother squeezed her hand. 'Never mind,' she said, 'it's all-age worship next week.' Hannah began to skip along the pavement. All-age worship usually meant some good songs, a much shorter time in chapel, and the service would probably include Mutt and Stu, two sheep puppets that the minister often brought to help explain what the Bible meant. Hannah and the other two children loved them, because they made the Bible interesting and easy to understand. Little did she know that her mother agreed with her…

Ben held his father's hand as they left their church. 'It's all-age worship next week!' called the children's group leader to Ben's departing back. 'Don't forget your recorder!' Ben and his father both groaned. Ben hated staying in church for the whole service, and was embarrassed that he had to play in the children's band. His father dreaded the monthly all-age worship that the church insisted was important to them and hated having to do things differently. He had not become a minister to lead whacky actions to silly songs and have babies screaming through what had to be a rushed exposition of the Bible. Perhaps Jane who was Brown Owl would do the talk as the uniformed organisations would be on church parade that day…

What do the children you know think about all-age worship?

> Dear God
>
> Thank you for my Salvation Army and for all the people who make it so special. Help our church to be a happy and caring and loving place. Amen
>
> Luke age 7

dealt with extremely sensitively for the family involved yet did not exclude younger children who were present. It was over in less than fifty minutes and I was left wanting more!

'The second service also included a baptism. Again, the music was well-chosen and the service sheet had been carefully planned to be helpful to children who could read. The vicar explained what each part of the service was about and invited children to sit on the chancel steps so that they could see and participate in the talk. They also went to the back of the church to watch the baptism at close range, and were so eager to get there that the vicar and family of the baby to be baptised had to fight their way through to the font. We were then told that there was nothing magical about the water; the special thing was what God would do. "It's just ordinary water in which this dinosaur has been swimming", said the vicar, removing a plastic toy from the font. The whole service took into account the needs and understanding of children, right down to the youngest there, and if anyone felt a little left out it was probably the adults!'

Not every church can achieve that level of child-friendly planning, and I would venture to say that neither of those churches could probably attain it every week, but in both cases the people who planned and led the services had considered who would be part of the congregation and had made it user-friendly even for 5 to 7s. Those who work with this age group week by week, and parents of children of this age, will breathe a sigh of relief and thank God if this happens each time children are in church for worship!

Children and Holy Communion
Not only are there differences of opinion across the denominations about this topic, but you will also find widely differing views within each denomination and even each church! Children and Holy Communion is an issue that brings out strong feelings on both sides of the debate. There are three main viewpoints:
- No child may take Communion.
- Some children may take Communion (usually dependent on whether or not they have been baptised).
- All children can take Communion.

Churches and denominations tend to arrive at their particular standpoint based on their beliefs about baptism, confirmation, what the Bible says, and on their history. Some denominations will have a policy that all churches must keep to, whilst others will allow individual congregations to make up their own minds. See the opposite page for real life examples that highlight the issues.

Many free churches have allowed children to take Communion for some time now. The Roman Catholic Church has made a child's first Communion to be a great event, happening any time from the age of about 7 upwards. In recent years there has been a change in the legislation governing the Church of England, so that children may be allowed to take Communion if first the diocesan bishop decides to implement the new regulations and then

All- age worship

All-age worship that helps children of this age to participate, whether 'up front' or in their seats, will include some of these characteristics:

- Recognition of the presence of children of this age
- Songs that have a good rhythm, understandable words and express a single concept
- Simple language and short sentences
- Concrete ideas, not abstract thoughts
- Story
- Activity
- Good acoustics and sight lines – or an invitation to 'come and see' when appropriate
- Visuals – both to illustrate talks and to accompany other aspects of worship, such as images to fit with prayer topics
- Short prayers that are clear and focused
- A relatively short Bible reading in a modern translation
- Good explanations about why things are being done
- Good links between different sections of the service
- Links to the world of 5 to 7s
- Opportunity to participate, such as being asked questions, invited to do some tasks – preferably by volunteering, asked for an opinion, invited to join in responses, asked to hold something or given something to take home as a reminder of the theme

Top Tips All-age worship

Nick Harding

An inspirational look at why all-age worship is not only desirable but do-able in your church! Explore some of the features of an all-age church and think about the different components of a worship service and how to use them. Plus practical pointers on issues such as planning, leadership and getting creative.

ISBN 978 1 84427 125 2

£2.99

the PCC of the church votes in favour of it and has their policy accepted by the bishop. However this can raise some difficult issues.

At what age is a child ready to take Communion? Opinions differ. The Orthodox Church will give bread dipped in wine to babies, yet other denominations would say that in order to take Communion a person must understand the meaning of Communion, and children are incapable of that. (It is highly likely that not all adults understand the meaning of this sacrament, but the assumption is often that age brings knowledge.)

Whatever your denomination you may have to face questions from parents about children and Communion. On the opposite page are some ideas to help you consider the implications of children being present during Communion, but not sharing in it fully, as well as other suggestions about how you prepare children for and teach about Communion.

Baptism

Traditionally a church-goer's view of baptism – how and when it should happen – was linked strongly to the denomination of the church to which they belonged. Those who were part of Anglican, Methodist, Roman Catholic or United Reformed churches saw baptism as a sacrament of God's grace and so young babies would be baptised by sprinkling with water. Those worshipping in Baptist or Pentecostal churches, for example, practised 'believers' baptism' by total immersion as a sign of faith and commitment to Jesus, which would not happen until adulthood or teenage years at least. Today the divisions are not always quite as clear as we find, for example, a growing number of Anglican churches with full-size baptisteries or those where parents are delaying baptism until their child is old enough to decide for themselves if and when they want to be baptised.

As the section on children and Communion points out, on deciding whether children may be admitted to Communion, the key question is often whether or not they have been baptised. Many churches that are now admitting children to Communion have specified a lower age limit of 7. So in these churches parents of children who have been dedicated may ask your help and advice in thinking through whether they should raise the issue of baptism with their child. Be ready for this by discussing the issue with your minister so that together you can help parents understand the different views. Make sure everyone is clear what the church believes and how you will put that into practice.

Equally if you are in a church where people are baptised as believers you may have children as young as 7 asking for baptism. Many churches would hold off until a child is older – perhaps around 12 years of age – but more and more children are asking at a younger age. It is not a decision that can be taken across the board – every child should be considered as an individual and, of course, their parents need to be involved at every stage. As well as discussing the ins and outs of allowing a 7-year-old to be baptised by immersion, consider too what might be the impact of denying baptism at this age.

Case studies – what would you do or say?

Talk about this with the other 5 to 7s leaders.

Ruth started to take Communion three months ago, not long after her seventh birthday. She loves it! Two weeks ago her family moved house and went to their new parish church. Ruth went up for Communion with her parents and was quite indignant when the vicar simply placed his hand on her head and prayed for God to bless her. She began to ask for the bread but her father quietened her, and whispered that they would explain to the vicar later. When they spoke to him after the service the vicar told them that the parish had never discussed the topic because he did not believe that it was right for children to take Communion. However, Church of England legislation says that once a child has been admitted to Communion they cannot be stopped from taking it, so the vicar will have to give Ruth Communion in future. This will no doubt lead to questions from other parents.

Stephen was baptised as a baby because his parents believed that it was 'the done thing' and his grandmother wanted a reason to bring out the white gown in which his father had been baptised 30 years before. Stephen's parents would not normally go to church, but whilst staying with friends who are Christians he would go to church with them. The Christian parents were keen that their son, Lee, should not be baptised until he could decide about it for himself. As baptism, rather than confirmation, is now the key factor in whether or not a child should be admitted to Communion, when the vicar announces that anyone who has been baptised can take bread and wine, it is Stephen, in church for only the second time in his life, who is allowed to participate in this way. Lee, the regular churchgoer, can only watch.

Dwayne and his family worship in a Baptist church where children over the age of 7 can take Communion but children under this age can take it if their parents agree, as long as they do not eat and drink 'in an unworthy manner' (see 1 Corinthians 11:27). So Dwayne, aged 5, tries hard to sit still while the bread and juice, as he calls it, are brought round. Is that what his mum expects of him when she says he has to 'be worthy'?

Millie has grown up in a Methodist church and has taken Communion since being very young. When asked what she enjoyed about church worship she answered, 'I like it when you get a little snack at the end of the service.' When quizzed more it became clear that this 'snack' was Communion. Why did she like it? 'Because if I'm hungry, it keeps me going until lunch!'

Jared has come to church with his friend Greg. His parents have never been churchgoers, and so it is all alien to him. As his Sunday group meets in the vestry where the Communion bread and wine are prepared, Jared watches with interest as the man pours a reddish-brown liquid into small glasses. 'Oh, sherry!' he comments. His group leader is now in a quandary: what should she do or say when Communion is brought round the church before the children leave?

Integration of children

For many years churches took the Victorian view of children, that they should be seen but not heard. Some still do today. You may be reading this with a sense of frustration that children are not really valued, never mind integrated into the life of the congregation in your church. Changing people's views takes time, but even a small movement of the rudder will eventually take a large ship to a different destination, and God, who longs for children to be accepted and valued even more than we do, is God, after all! Be patient, but be persistent, too, in raising the profile of children and families and helping others to see what more could be done. As well as championing the needs of children, point out what children bring to the church family!

Listed on page 153 are some of the characteristics of a church that integrates children well. You might ask your church council to consider these at some stage and discuss the role of children in church.

Taking note of children's views

Some churches have 'children's councils' where the views of under 11s are not just heard but sought. Adults often think they know what children want, but it is good to ask them and to allow them to shape the way things are done in church. There may be some surprises! Without needing a formal 'meeting' this can be done through questionnaires and discussions. It should not happen too often – children love being asked their opinions, but soon tire of it on the grounds that they have already been asked!

Some would say that 5-, 6- and 7-year-olds are too young to be asked about things such as this. But they will have very clear views (often of what they do not like rather than what they do!) if we can but ask the right questions or pick up clues, perhaps even from their play. Ask the parents of this age group to listen in if ever their children play 'church' at home. We can learn much from what they include, what they say and from their tone of voice!

As well as asking the views of children they should be given opportunity to know what is happening in the life of the congregation and to participate in important things at an appropriate level.

Pete is father to 7-year-old Rebecca. He is also the church treasurer. So when telling the congregation about the church's forthcoming gift day he includes all the children, suggesting that they might give some of their pocket money. Rebecca has taken this to heart and puts a small amount of money aside each week until the gift day. When it comes to the time to make their gifts Rebecca beams as she puts her gift of money in the box.
The church attended by 6-year-old Simon and his family is due to be pulled down and rebuilt. During a 24-hour period of prayer for the project, one hour is set aside especially for children. The first thing they do during the time is to walk round the building looking at all the cracks in the walls so that the children understand why there is a need for a new church. At the end of the time each child takes home a prayer cube to help them continue to pray for different

5-7s and Communion

Here are some ideas to help you consider the implications of children being present during Communion, but not sharing in it fully, as well as other suggestions about how you teach about Communion and prepare children for it.

If children are present at a Communion service but not taking part

- Ensure that they understand what it is about: a time to remember Jesus' death and to celebrate his coming back to life.

- Explain what the different parts of the service are about:

  that people shake hands or hug one other as a way of praying for God's peace for each other

  that the bread and wine or juice remind us of the special things that Jesus said when he ate a final supper with his friends, and the special things that happened when Jesus died on the cross

  that the prayers are a way of saying 'thank you' to God for all that he has done for us.

- Help them to understand that this is a very special part of the service for many grown ups, who are often very quiet while they think about it.

- If children are going to receive a blessing, explain what will happen and what is expected of them.

- Explain why they cannot take Communion at this stage, and when they will be able to do so. ('When you are older' may not be enough to satisfy the curiosity of some!)

If your church prints its own service sheet or uses PowerPoint for the service order you might find it helpful to include some simple line drawings or symbols that represent the different important parts of the service. The Communion Cube (Church House Publishing) is designed to help children understand the meaning of the Communion service.

To prepare children to take Communion

Your denomination may have guidelines about this. Anglican churches have to present an outline of how they will go about it before they are given permission to admit children to Communion. Generally speaking children need to be aware of the same things as outlined above, and the reasons behind them, but will also need to be reassured about how to take Communion: whether to stand or kneel, whether they will be given bread or a wafer, if they can touch the chalice if one is used, when to go back to their seats or details of any special practices your church may have.

aspects of the project and Simon solemnly gets this out every evening before he goes to bed, sometimes saying a short prayer himself and sometimes asking whoever puts him to bed to pray instead.

Leroy and his family worship at St Catherine's church, the largest church in a busy suburb. It is to become a joint benefice with St Bartholomew's, the neighbouring parish church which Amy and her Mum attend regularly. The two congregations come together for a day of talking and sharing their vision for how they can work together more to help others in the area to know Jesus. Children are fully involved and have their own sessions to think about how they can be God's people in the places where they live, play and go to school. Leroy's favourite part of the day is where everyone – all ages together – shows photographs that they have taken of the places where they like to spend time. He shows a picture of the library. Amy says she enjoys lunch most of all, when there are lots of different things to try. But at the end of it she still thinks her mum's rice and peas taste best!

What can you do to help your church involve and welcome 5 to 7s in decision-making processes? What can you do to help the group to understand the major issues affecting the church?

Festivals

Christmas is often the time when those responsible for planning the content of services or groups despair because 'they know this story – it's the same every year!' They do, but the younger ones at least are still at the stage of enjoying repetition. Part of the appeal of listening to the narratives of Christmas is the familiarity of the story. Children who have heard the story several times before know what comes next, and this can give young children who are constantly dealing with new things, a sense of achievement.

This is not just a good time for children already in church but a prime time to draw in those who do not usually attend. It is also a wonderful opportunity to tell something of God's good news to children who would not normally have any contact with the Christian message. Here is a great opening to tell them about Jesus! Within the church there are a number of possible events or services that will be enjoyed by children of this age.

- Christingle services have grown in popularity and many churches now hold one each year. Most take place before Christmas but they can be held up to Epiphany.
- Crib services are usually held on Christmas Eve, when a nativity scene is created and the baby placed in the manger. The service will include simple and well known carols, and again the atmosphere may well be heightened by use of candles and dimmed electric lighting.
- Nativity plays are more often associated with school, where there is a necessity to give every child a part. As a result the narrative may be embroidered so much that the basic facts are swamped. Unless there is a strong Christian influence in the school it may simply be told as the story of Mary and Joseph's baby being born, without reference to

Signs that a church welcomes children

A church that integrates children well will have many of the following characteristics:

Acceptance of the fact that:
- children are as much valued members of the church family as adults are
- children will behave like children and not like adults!
- children are still learning, and what they offer may not be perfect
- children have lots to offer in worship
- the contributions that children make to worship are not about performance but about leading the congregation to worship God

Willingness to listen:
- to God
- to all ages equally
- to those who work with children or who speak on behalf of children
- to children themselves

Willingness to take on board the practical implications of integrating children such as:
- using more visuals – for talks, prayers, etc
- singing some songs that are suitable for younger children – ie those that have less words, only one theme, appropriate concepts and are easily remembered
- producing service sheets that use child-friendly fonts and print sizes, simple wording and appropriate illustrations
- encouraging children to either sit at the front so that they can see better, or to have freedom to roam a little if sitting still is not easy
- encouraging children to come to the appropriate place and take a good look when there are important things happening such as a baptism
- explaining in simple terms the significance of an event such as baptism
- having a welcome team who look out for new families with young children and point them to toilets, good places to sit, crèche, children's groups etc

Good integration of all ages, as children are no more and no less important than any other age group

Jesus being the Son of God. At this age children are still happy to dress up and will often enjoy taking part in a retelling of the Bible story. Make the most of this and tell the nativity story accurately, making it clear who Jesus is and what God's part was in it all. Be as creative as possible whilst sticking to the truth!

- A Christmas fun day, perhaps held on a Saturday early in December, will endear you to any parent (except those who are involved as helpers!) as you provide them with the opportunity to sort out those shopping purchases that need to be bought in secret! But much more than that, it will give children a growing sense of anticipation about the real Christmas. For more ideas see *More Christmas Wrapped up*

Easter is a very different festival from Christmas. That is obvious, but we must recognise that unlike Christmas, where the Bible story has huge appeal to children just as the secular side does, the Christian side of Easter (foot-washing and death on a cross) will never appeal to young children in quite the same way as the fluffy chicks and baby rabbits put across by the secular world. There is harshness to Easter. As we teach about Easter we should consider that teaching about suffering is never easy. Yet without explaining that Jesus died on the cross we are not telling the whole story. Children at the lower end of this age bracket may not yet have learnt the painful truth that death is the end. Without knowing that, the resurrection loses its power! If children grasp the wonder of the resurrection it may raise questions for them when a close family member dies. If this happens, talk with the child's relatives and with your minister before tackling the issue with the child.

A growing number of churches run Easter activities for children. The following would be suitable for 5 to 7s:

- An Easter holiday club during Holy week, an activity session of simple crafts linked to Easter themes, a special event on Good Friday that might involve walking through the events between Palm Sunday and Easter Day, plus crafts, story, and songs. It could culminate in an all-age service.
- Breakfast before all-age worship on Easter Day.

It is far harder to draw in children from outside the church for Easter events than for Christmas. But that fact should not deter us; perhaps, except for breakfast, the above ideas would work just as well with children not used to church. If they come however, we will need to tell the story clearly and simply. It will be even less well known than Christmas. For more details see *Easter Cracked.*

Pentecost is sometimes considered hard for children to understand, perhaps because some adults are also confused or cautious about the Holy Spirit and his work. Children of this age need concrete ideas to help them grasp the concept of someone who cannot be seen yet is at work in powerful ways. When Jesus talked to Nicodemus about those born of the Spirit he used the example of the wind, which cannot be seen but the effect of which is clearly visible (John 3:8). This is a useful picture with 5 to 7s who will have no doubt about the presence and impact of the wind, whether it is in blowing the washing dry on a line or flying a kite.

Resources

All at £9.99!

Christmas Wrapped Up!

978 1 85999 795 6

More Christmas Wrapped Up!

978 1 84427 261 7

These two titles for Christmas are packed full of top-quality material combining years of SU experience with exciting new ideas. They will help churches get the most out of Christmas this year and for years to come.

Easter Cracked

978 1 84427 189 4

Easter Cracked is a vital resource for churches hoping to make the most of the opportunities they have to reach out during Easter. Contains services, craft, drama and more to use with all-ages.

Celebrations Sorted

ISBN 978 1 84427 182 5

Celebrations Sorted is packed full of ideas for churches to use at times of celebration in the church calendar (other than Christmas or Easter). Contains service outlines, craft, drama, assemblies, creative prayer and more.

Jesus used similarly helpful, concrete descriptions of the Holy Spirit as a comforter and teacher, which will help children to grasp more about the Spirit. It is perhaps easier to explain the fruit of the Spirit and the gifts of the Spirit, but the idea that the Holy Spirit lives inside those who follow Jesus may cause problems. As literal thinkers this age group may have big questions such as 'How does he get in there?' or 'What does he eat?' They'll probably be confused or scared by the idea of a person or force at work in them. Stories of how the Holy Spirit helped the disciples to be brave, to talk about Jesus, to heal people and so on, followed by words such as, 'and he will help us today too, if we ask him' will enable children to grasp why the Holy Spirit is special and important.

Harvest is a festival most primary schools will celebrate. Children will have a chance to think about the many things we enjoy and the need to share them. This is an easy festival for 5 to 7s to understand because it focuses on concrete ideas of food, nature and the world around us. But usually little is done in churches beyond celebration services and suppers. A Light Night as an alternative to Halloween is another option for this time of year. See *Celebrations Sorted!* for more details.

It is worth thinking too about Father's Day, and what the commercial world calls Mother's Day, but what the church has traditionally celebrated as Mothering Sunday. Both days present great opportunities to talk about God's care for us and is an opportunity to celebrate family life. But in a world where divorce and disease divide and spoil families, we will need to choose our words carefully in order to avoid compounding the pain that some children suffer because the relevant parent is either no longer at home or not alive.

Pastoral care

We may not think of pastoral care in relation to 5 to 7s but there will be times in their lives when they need specific support and help. As adults we might categorise these times as good (such as the birth of a sibling, changing class or moving house) or bad experiences (such as the illness or death of a close family member, or the separation or divorce of parents). To the child they may feel very different. The birth of a baby may mean that they get less time and attention from their parents, especially if they have been the only child up to this point. Moving house may mean leaving friends and changing school, whilst the death of a grandparent who lives some distance away may hardly impact them, but devastate their parents. There may be opposite reactions to the same events from different family members. For example, a parent will be very happy to be remarrying, but their child may be devastated that this really does mean that Mum and Dad will never be together again.

Our role is to listen, to try to understand what they are experiencing and how they are reacting to it. We need to accept any behaviour changes that may result which are not just naughtiness and help the child return to normality as soon as possible. We must also offer unconditional love and support throughout the time, and help other children to deal sensitively with them. It may also be that trauma in one child's life affects others and so we need to offer reassurance to the wider group.

More than that, on a weekly basis we need to be aware of each child's home and family circumstances so that we do not use the wrong words such as, 'Take this home to Mummy and Daddy' when they live with just one parent. Do not only give examples of children from one type of family.

School visits

Increasing numbers of churches are creating events and presentations to which local schools can be invited: Christmas presentations; Easter presentations; discovery visits about the building and its history; discovery visits about Christian worship and special occasions, perhaps acting out a wedding or baptism, and discovery visits about the life of a particular Christian or group associated with that church.

Talk to your local school about what might work before getting too far with plans, but when you approach them have a clear idea of what you could offer rather than starting with a blank sheet of paper.

Resources

Resource books

101 Ideas for Creative Prayers	Judith Merrell	Scripture Union
Anyone Can Tell a Story	Bob Hartman	Lion Publishing
Better Than Hallowe'en	Nick Harding	Church House Publishing
Bible Alive	Penny Boshoff	Scripture Union
Celebrations Sorted		Scripture Union
Children's Guide to the Bible	Robert Willoughby	Scripture Union
Christmas Wrapped Up		Scripture Union
Come and Join the Celebration	John Muir & Betty Pedley	Church House Publishing
Creative Assemblies for KS1	Heather Butler	Scripture Union
Easter Cracked		Scripture Union
Here's One I Made Earlier	Kathryn Copsey	Scripture Union
Here's Another One I Made Earlier	Christine Orme	Scripture Union
More Christmas Wrapped Up		Scripture Union
New Ideas for Creative Prayer	Judith Merrell	Scripture Union
Over 300 Games for all Occasions	Patrick Goodland	Scripture Union
Ready Steady Assembly!	Claire Derry & Helen Franklin	Scripture Union
Telling the Bible	Bob Hartman	Lion Publishing

Reading the Bible with 5-7s

Bible Timeline	Scripture Union
The Big Bible Storybook	Scripture Union
Join In, Jump On! (various titles)	Scripture Union
The Little Bible Storybook	Scripture Union

Books to help children know more of God

Friends with Jesus (booklet)		Scripture Union
So, Who Is God?	Robert Willoughby	Scripture Union
The Strong Tower	Robert Harrison	Scripture Union
Y God?	Steve Hutchinson	Scripture Union

Eye level club materials (especially for children not used to church)

Awesome (John's gospel) – book and DVD   Scripture Union

Clues 2 Use (Jesus Quest DVD)   Scripture Union

High Five (Mark's gospel)   Scripture Union

Streetwise (Luke's gospel) – book and DVD   Scripture Union

Rocky Road (Moses)   Scripture Union

Target Challenge (Olympics)   Scripture Union

Scripture Union Holiday Clubs

Champion's Challenge (Luke's gospel)

Desert Detectives (the Bible)

Expedition Force (Easter narratives in Matthew)

Landlubbers (Philippians and Acts)

Pyramid Rock (Joseph's story)

Seaside Rock (Peter's story)

Wastewatchers (John's gospel and Genesis 1)

Light material (for 5-7s groups in church) is called Splash!

Scripture Union Top Tips series

All Age worship   Nick Harding

Growing Faith with Families   Pauline Burdett

Handling Difficult Behaviour   Graham Finch

Reaching Unchurched Children   Helen Franklin

Welcoming Children of Other Faiths   Gill Marchant, Andrew Smith

Welcoming Special Children   Denise Abrahall

Encouraging faith to grow   Ruth Hassall, Piers Lane

Prompting Prayer   Sarah Bingham, Vicki Blyth

Sharing Bible stories   Sue Brown, Andy Gray, Gill Marchant

Explaining the cross   Helen Franklin, Steve Hutchinson, Robert Willoughby

Communicating God in non-book ways   Kathryn Copsey, Jean Elliott

To help you think further about work with children

The Adventure Begins	Terry Clutterham	Scripture Union
Children Finding Faith	Francis Bridger	Scripture Union
Children in the Church?	Betty Pedley, John Muir	National Society / CHP
Every Child A Chance to Choose	Penny Frank	Children's Ministry
Godly Play	Jerome W Berryman	Augsburg (Minneapolis)
Kid's Culture	Nick Harding	Scripture Union
Leading Children	Penny Frank	Children's Ministry
Reaching Children	Paul Butler	Scripture Union
Running Christian Groups in Schools	Esther Bailey	Scripture Union
The Schools Work Handbook	Emlyn Williams	Scripture Union
The Story of the Book	Terence Copley	Scripture Union

Government documents and publications

Every Child Matters (www.everychildmatters.gov.uk)

Safe from Harm (access via www.ofsted.gov.uk)

Churches Child Protection Advisory Services (www.ccpas.co.uk)

DVDs

Jesus Quest (the 'Jesus' film for children)	Agapé

CDs

Bitesize Bible Songs (also available as downloads)	Scripture Union
Light for Everyone	Scripture Union
Reach Up!	Scripture Union

Other useful resources

The Baptism Cube	Church House Publishing
The Communion Cube	Church House Publishing
The Lord's Prayer Cube	Church House Publishing